Elijah's

REVOLUTION

*The Call to Passion
and Sacrifice for
Radical Change*

JIM W. GOLL
LOU ENGLE

Treasure House

An Imprint of
Destiny Image® Publishers, Inc.
P.O. Box 310
Shippensburg, PA 17257-0310

"For where your treasure is, there will your heart be also."
Matthew 6:21

ISBN 0-7684-2057-1
Library of Congress Catalog Card Number 2002-141113

For Worldwide Distribution
Printed in the U.S.A.

First Printing: 2002   Second Printing: 2002

This book and all other Destiny Image, Revival Press, MercyPlace, Fresh Bread, Destiny Image Fiction, and Treasure House books are available at Christian bookstores and distributors worldwide.

For a U.S. bookstore nearest you, call **1-800-722-6774.**
For more information on foreign distributors, call **717-532-3040.**
Or reach us on the Internet:
www.destinyimage.com

Acknowledgment and Dedication

For every book that comes forth, there is a host of people to thank as each one is a "team effort." We owe a great debt of gratitude to our respective families—especially our sacrificing wives who hold the fort down for us as we carry this message far and wide. So first we say thanks to Michal Ann Goll and to Therese Engle for being our perfect helpers! We also wish to acknowledge the staffs and prayer warriors at Ministry to the Nations, Harvest Rock Church, Harvest International Ministries, and The Call Revolution for their faithful support. We need you! Thank You, Lord, for these teams that we get to partner with!

Next, we wish to thank the great group of servants at Destiny Image. Your commitment to excellence and purity of content has come forth like a shining light once again. Thanks for your creativity and patience with us in doing this project. Thanks for believing in this message and thanks for believing in us.

We wish to dedicate this book to the next generation of "Nazirites" and passionate warriors for the cause of Christ.

This book is about your future. This book is about our purpose in God together—The Call to Passion and Sacrifice for Radical Change! We dedicate this book to the youth of America and the nations in hope that a genuine Elijah Revolution will come to pass for Jesus Christ's sake.

Jim W. Goll and Lou Engle

Endorsements

"God is uniting the generations in a call for holy revolution. This is not rhetoric-it is a sincere, passionate declaration backed up by lifestyles of consecration and service. This book will fuel the flame of change in your life! I highly recommend it!"

—Robert Stearns, Executive Director
Eagles Wings Ministries
New York City

"Prepare to be enlightened and get ready to be challenged as you read this powerful forward-looking book! Two dynamic men of God, Lou Engle and Jim Goll, have given us a vision of the trans-generational anointing of the future church that is a prophetic, passionate statement of the heart of God in this hour. You will be enlightened by the insights into Scripture that the Lord has revealed to them in relation to the "now" issues facing the church. You will also be challenged to come up higher in your commitment to be "possessed by God," so that He may have a people through whom

He can bring revival to America and the nations of the world."

—Jane Hansen, President/CEO
Aglow International

"In all probability the generation anointed by God to catalyze a worldwide spiritual earthquake has already been born. This book is destined to prepare the whole body of Christ to receive this radical outpouring of God's power here on earth!"

—C. Peter Wagner, Chancellor
Wagner Leadership Institute

"At times a book is written in such a manner that when you read it, it reads you!

This book coauthored by my friends Jim Goll and Lou Engle will fan a fire in your bones that you will not be able to put out. Let's join "The Call" so that it will be heard far and wide recruiting a generation of passionate, sacrificial servants who will usher in radical change."

—Mike Bickle, Director
International House of Prayer of Kansas City

"Lou Engle and Jim Goll are role models for me-they are men of courage, spiritual passion and integrity. I share their commitment to raising up a younger generation of radical young believers who will not let the church be controlled by our secular culture-or by impotent religious tradition. This book will fan your zeal into a blazing fire."

—J. Lee Grady, Editor
Charisma magazine

"You would expect a book entitled 'Elijah's Revolution' to be characterized by extreme passion, prophetic insight and the all-consuming fire of God. You would expect it to inspire change, impart zeal, infuse with power, and incite revival. Thankfully, you would be right! And if you know them as I do, you would also expect it to be written by individuals like Jim Goll and Lou Engle, who embody all of the above. Prepare to be transformed!"

—Dutch Sheets
Colorado Springs, CO

"*The Call DC* was a powerful movement of God's Spirit to awaken a new generation to the unquenchable pursuit of Him. In *Elijah's Revolution*, Lou Engle and Jim Goll cast an exciting vision for how this generation can grow into an irresistible force—abandoned to His will and unwilling to compromise with America's fallen culture. I stand with our youth today—they are our leaders of tomorrow."

—Dr. Bill Bright, Founder and President
Campus Crusade for Christ International

Contents

Foreword

All eyes fell upon New York City that September day of 2001 as the World Trade Center lay decimated by terrorists. Prognosticators all across the world agreed "things would never be the same again" in our nation. God used that tragic "9-11" event to rouse both believer and unbeliever alike. That date will stand forever as a prophetic plumb line drawn in the sands of time.

The book of First Chronicles tells us about the "sons of Issachar who understood the times and knew what to do" (1 Chron. 12:32). Now, more than ever, we need God's sons and daughters arising in this hour to deliver God's strategy and solution to us for such a time as this.

Lou Engle and Jim Goll have been pressed by God to issue one such mandate. I know because I have watched them. I know their lives intimately. I have seen them weep and pray and fast and seek the God of our fathers relentlessly for years on end. I have seen them struggle to birth what God is asking of those who passionately love God and are desperate for more of Him.

I believe they have obeyed and are now issuing forth a revolutionary call. It began long before "9-11," but only increases in intensity as each moment ticks by. It is a call to those who are bone weary of the hedonism, humanism, selfishness, and greed that surround us every day...even within the church. It is a call to those grieved by the lawlessness of our nation, the hardness of sin, and the destruction of lives from the inside out. It is a call to those who may sense more of God's presence in their lives than ever before, yet suffer a great discontentment with "the way things are."

It is a call to a revolution of *the heart*. It is a cry to young, old, and in-between. It is a call to elders and nursing babes...to housewives and dissatisfied teens...to fathers and factory workers...to any and all with a heart attuned to the Spirit of God.

You will find this book is not a blood-pumping, quick fix text for a generation immersed in chaos and clamor. Rather it is a summons to a Spirit-birthed lifestyle consumed by the love of God that can readily change the course of human events. It is a call for history makers—a call for the "nobodies," who, when breathed upon by God, become Gideons of great consequence; it is a call for the "somebodies," who, when breathed upon by God, are struck down like Paul from their mighty horses and given new eyes to see and new weapons of humility in supernatural power that will change the world.

It begins right here, right now, as you read this book. Let God breathe upon its every word, and illuminate to you your place and destiny in this revolution. Let an "Elijah revelation" flood your soul and cause you to think like God in this hour. Let passion for Jesus consume your flesh and give you a braveheart spirit that will answer this call in the way destined only for you. Say "yes" with your heart and your actions...and you will find yourself stepping into a place God has ordained for you throughout all time.

For this cause,

—Dr. Ché H. Ahn
Harvest Rock Church
Pasedena, CA

Introduction

Let me give you a brief sketch of the contents of this coauthored book by Lou Engle and myself, Jim W. Goll. Lou and I have had the wonderful opportunity of interacting over the last several years on issues concerning the historic moves of the Holy Spirit as it pertains to revival. A deepened hunger from the Lord keeps on grabbing hold of our souls until we can no longer just read about the great moves of God in the past. We have been consumed to such a degree that we have to do something about it now! That is where this book comes in and why it is burning in your hands as you hold it.

Elijah's Revolution is an attempt to bring to you in print some of the pounding sounds that echo in our hearts. We want to see a whole generation arise that will passionately sacrifice the temporal pleasures of this life so as to embrace *The Call* of God to seize the moment in which we live. Do you want to see a radical change take place in the church and societies as a whole? If you do, then the contents of this book will fan that fire into even a greater flame.

Since Lou's and my heart beat with such a similar sound, we decided to join forces and do this work together. Therefore, it is composed in a "we" tense. The message of this book is not an "I" and "me" thing. It is something that our Lord has deposited within us together. Having the privilege of both being on the same apostolic team, Harvest International Ministries, it only made sense to attempt to pen this message together.

So read on! Get infected with a radical passion for our lovely savior that will propel you to join the cries of multitudes of others—"Is there not a cause in the land?" Our answer is a resounding yes! Let *Elijah's Revolution* come forth for Jesus Christ sake!

—Jim W. Goll
Ministry to the Nations

Part One

This Is the Time...

Chapter One

...For the Call to Revolution

By 5:30 in the morning on Saturday, September 2, 2000, the National Mall in Washington, DC was already buzzing with the presence of 270,000 people. Thousands more were arriving every minute. Before the end of the day a crowd estimated at 400,000—mostly zealous Christian young people—jammed the Mall for an event unlike any other in recent memory. *The Call DC* brought together youth and adults from all over the U.S. and many other nations, summoning them to burn with passion for Jesus and an all-consuming desire to turn America back to God.[1]

Although the worship was awesome, this assembly had not come just to sing songs. Although the speakers were dynamic and challenging, this massive gathering had not come to listen to preaching. *They had come to pray.*

This was not a day of celebration. It was not a feast, but a fast! *The Call DC* was a solemn assembly in the spirit of that called forth in the Book of Joel:

> *"Yet even now," declares the Lord, "return to Me with all your heart, and with fasting, weeping, and mourning;*

*and rend your heart and not your garments." Now return
to the Lord your God, for He is gracious and compassionate, slow to anger, abounding in lovingkindness, and
relenting of evil....Blow a trumpet in Zion, consecrate a
fast, proclaim a solemn assembly, gather the people, sanctify the congregation, assemble the elders, gather the children and the nursing infants* (Joel 2:12-13,15-16a).

The Call's vision statement was clear. "The Call is a
solemn assembly bringing together two generations for the
purpose of praying and fasting for the revival and transformation of our cities and our nation."[2] We were focused. We
had our aim clearly defined!

For 12 straight hours young people and adults alike
wept and worshiped, confessed and repented, and fasted and
prayed, calling on Almighty God with desperation to pour
out His Spirit in a new "great awakening" that would shake
America to her very foundations. One specific focus of *The
Call DC* was to challenge those attending to commit themselves to a 40-day fast to pray for the United States, particularly in view of the upcoming national elections. Much of
the "platform ministry"—from the worship to the prayer and
intercession—was led by young people themselves. We envi-
sioned, but we empowered them to lead.

September 2, 2000, marked a spiritual "watershed" in
America's history. The United States faces a moral and spiritual crisis of unprecedented proportions. Decades of neglect, disobedience, and passivity by many in the Church have
produced a "cultural Christianity" that lacks revelation and is
devoid of true spiritual power. Immorality and worldliness
have made steady inroads into the lives of countless believers.
Rationalism and humanism rule in the majority of colleges
and universities across the land. Landmark legislation and
court decisions have legalized abortion on demand and all but
removed the Church's prophetic voice from the public arena.

Hollywood and the television and music industries fill the theaters, stadiums, auditoriums, and airwaves with all kinds of filth, immorality, and godless philosophies. As a result, the nation stands at a crossroads: either turn back to God or face greater deterioration and ultimately His judgment.

Critical times call for a radical response from the people of God. Traditional means, methods, and modes of thought are insufficient to meet the needs of the present hour. A more drastic approach is required. In every generation God summons forth Nazirites[3] from within His people—"separated" men and women who are satisfied with nothing less than undivided devotion to Christ, uncompromising obedience to His will, and unflinching engagement with a culture that is hostile to the things of God. *The Call DC* was merely one visible expression of this summons, a great cross-generational move of God in this day and age that can only be described as revolutionary.

A YOUTH EXTRAVAGANZA THAT WILL ROCK THE NATIONS

Revolutions rarely begin suddenly. Instead, they grow up over time as people become less and less satisfied with conditions as they are. One incident leads to another and tensions mount until finally one catalytic event becomes the flash point that propels them into action. The American Revolution did not occur overnight. Among other things, it arose because of a long series of actions by the British Parliament that many colonists felt were attacks on their civil liberties. Discontent and unrest grew until April 1775 when clashes between colonial militia and British regulars at Concord and Lexington, Massachusetts, became the flash point that sparked the colonies into open rebellion.

A spiritual revolution is underway in America, and it is already going global. The Holy Spirit is the instigator and He is doing a mighty work in the midst of God's people. Like any other revolution, the decay of the moral climate had been building up for some time.

Many people remember *Stand in the Gap*, the Promise Keepers-sponsored meeting on October 4, 1997, which brought hundreds of thousands of men from every denomination and walk of life together on the Mall in Washington, DC. Businessmen and bikers, engineers and architects, doctors and lawyers, students and teachers stood side by side for hours and worshiped, confessed, repented, and prayed together. It was a seminal event.

One year earlier, in November 1996, Jim Goll had a dream that was prophetically related to these mass gatherings in the nation's capital.

> I heard an audible voice which said, "Out of the belly of the Promise Keepers movement will come forth a youth extravaganza that will rock the nations. The stadiums will be filled. The stadiums will be filled as out of the belly of the Promise Keepers movement comes forth a youth extravaganza that will rock the nations."

> I awoke from this dream to the awareness of the presence of God permeating the bedroom. Immediately I was catapulted into an open vision where I saw a massive outdoor football stadium filled with young people who were radically worshiping God. Beams of laser light crisscrossed the sky and came together to form a huge cross that was high and lifted up above the stadium. At the same time an enormous screen at one end of the stadium was displaying a graphic multimedia presentation of the crucifixion of Christ. As a hammer pounded nails through the wrists of Jesus, in the background I heard people singing "Didn't He," an old song

from the Jesus Movement of the 1970s, with the words, "And the hammer fell on the wooden nails..."

As all this was occuring, the spirit of conviction of sin began falling upon the young people, and they started crying out to the Lord for mercy and screaming, "What must I do to be saved?" It was then that I heard aloud in the room once again the words, "Out of the belly of the Promise Keepers movement will come forth a youth extravaganza that will rock the nations."

At that time I had no idea at all that a year later the Promise Keepers would be holding *Stand in the Gap* in Washington, DC, or that in another three years hundreds of thousands of young people would gather at the same place for *The Call DC*.

"A MILLION KIDS ON THE MALL"

Not long after *Stand in the Gap*, Lou Engle was preaching in Phoenix, Arizona, on the subject of the Nazirite vow and how a modern Nazirite generation would arise and be "the hinge of history." During that meeting, in a divine encounter completely separate from Jim's, Lou received a prophetic vision of a youth counterpart to *Stand in the Gap* that could put a million young people on the Mall in Washington, DC. Caught up with this vision, Lou began preaching it at youth conferences all over the country.

A year and a half later, in the spring of 1999, a nameless, faceless woman who had never heard Lou preach came up to him and asked, "Lou, have you ever thought about putting a million kids on the Mall in DC to pray for a massive shift of revival in America?" When Lou answered that he had been preaching this vision for a year and a half, she said, "I want to give you $100,000 as seed money to help launch it."

This was one week before the shootings at Columbine High School in Littleton, Colorado. Every revolution has a flash point, and for the spiritual revolution now underway among America's youth, that flash point was Columbine.

Although Lou was excited about the financial support and this confirmation of his vision, he really did not know how to begin to put it all together. One thing quickly led to another. When Lou shared this experience a couple of days later with two prayer leaders from the East Coast, they advised him to get in touch with Bart Pierce, pastor of the Rock City Church in Baltimore, Maryland. As the organizer of *Washington for Jesus,* a prayer event that drew 800,000 people to the National Mall in 1988, Bart had the experience and the contacts to help realize Lou's vision.

At first Lou did not see how in the world he could get connected with Bart Pierce. The very next week, however, Lou and his family were in the Baltimore-Washington area to attend a wedding and enjoy a few days of vacation. On Sunday Lou preached at a church in Philadelphia. Afterwards, the pastor came up and said, "Lou, I was in a pastor's meeting and met Bart Pierce. When I told him that you were preaching at my church, he said, 'I need to meet with him.' "

The very next day Lou found himself in Bart Pierce's office where they discussed Lou's vision for putting a million kids on the Mall in Washington. As it turned out, Rock City Church was at that very time hosting a large prayer gathering where many different churches had come together to pray for God to break the hard shell of Washington, DC. One of the speakers was Dutch Sheets, who shared his vision of young people coming to the nation's capital and of revival fire falling on Washington.

During that same meeting, Bart Pierce invited Lou to share his vision before the 3,000 people who were attending that night. One of those in the congregation was a man with whom Lou had covenanted in 1993 to connect Washington, DC and Los Angeles, where Lou lived. Later this same man had helped organize and manage the *Stand in the Gap* meeting on the National Mall in 1997.

For a long time God had been at work in different places imparting into many different hearts threads of His vision and desire for America and for this present generation. Now He was weaving those threads together into a tapestry of divine purpose, calling His people not just to revival but to radical revolution—*Elijah's Revolution.*

RESTORING THE HEARTS OF THE FATHERS AND THE CHILDREN

The closing verses of the last book of the Old Testament contain a remarkable prophecy. After spending three chapters taking the Israelites to task for their public and private sins and for rebelling against God, Malachi ends with these encouraging words from the Lord:

> *Remember the law of Moses My servant, even the statutes and ordinances which I commanded him in Horeb for all Israel. Behold, I am going to send you Elijah the prophet before the coming of the great and terrible day of the Lord. And he will restore the hearts of the fathers to their children, and the hearts of the children to their fathers, lest I come and smite the land with a curse* (Malachi 4:4-6).

First, the Lord charges the people to "remember the law of Moses" as found in the Pentateuch, the first five books of the Bible, and as embodied specifically in the Ten Commandments, which they were violating. Then He promises to send "Elijah the prophet" to usher in a period of restoration that will turn the hearts of the fathers and the children to each other and back to God. This transgenerational awakening will occur "before the coming of the great and terrible day of the Lord" and will prevent the "curse" of God's judgment from smiting the land or even reverse it if necessary.

The Gospels of Matthew and Luke make it clear that John the Baptist was the historical fulfillment of God's promise in Malachi to "send...Elijah the prophet."[4] John was also the prophetic forerunner who prepared the way for the coming of Christ. Through His life, death, and resurrection, Jesus certainly turned the hearts of many fathers (and mothers) and children back to the heavenly Father and inaugurated an age of grace in which the judgment of God is averted to give everyone an opportunity to hear the gospel and repent.

However, the nature of biblical prophecy is such that in many instances there may be more than one fulfillment. In Malachi 4:5, for example, the phrase "the great and terrible day of the Lord" is a common prophetic expression understood to refer not so much to Christ's first coming as to His second coming. In this context Malachi 4:5-6 can be seen as prophesying a *spirit* of Elijah that will arise in the endtimes, igniting a transgenerational awakening that will turn the hearts of the fathers and the children back to God and prepare the way for the triumphant return of Christ.

Already there are signs that this has begun to happen. *Stand in the Gap* was powerful and significant evidence that the Promise Keepers movement has an anointing of turning the hearts of the fathers to the children and back to the Father. This anointing even now has moved beyond the borders of the United States and entered Europe and other lands. Many Christian leaders believe it will continue to progress across the globe as a forerunner ministry that is part of a latter-day fulfillment of Malachi's prophecy.

Then, "out of the belly of the Promise Keepers movement" and sparked by Columbine, came *The Call DC,* one of several indicators signifying the arising of a new generation of "children" whose hearts are being turned back both to their earthly fathers and to their heavenly Father.

The Call DC was not a one-time event. It was a catalyst that opened a door to new beginnings. On September 22, 2001, *The Call New England* drew an estimated 50,000 believers to Boston's City Hall Plaza. For 12 hours participants fasted, repented for the sins of both the Church and the nation, and prayed for revival, spiritual transformation, and ethnic, gender, and generational reconciliation in every area of society. This solemn assembly was especially urgent and timely in the wake of the horrific terrorist attacks on New York City and Washington just 11 days earlier.

As the Spirit of God leads, plans are underway for similar gatherings in New York City (June 29, 2002), Kansas City (Dec. 31, 2002), Dallas, Los Angeles, Nashville, San Diego and other cities as well as international locations such as the Philippines (November 30, 2001), England (July 13, 2002), Korea (November 2002), and Germany. This radical voice crying in the wilderness is going to spread like a prairie grass fire across the nations of the earth.

A revolution is underway today in a spiritual and moral environment that resembles in many respects that which existed in Israel when the original prophet Elijah made his mark. How did Elijah bring a revolution about?

FROM MOUNT CARMEL TO MOUNT HOREB

Elijah first bursts abruptly onto the scene in Israel with a pronouncement of drought as God's judgment for the nation's sins: "Now Elijah the Tishbite, who was of the settlers of Gilead, said to Ahab, 'As the Lord, the God

of Israel lives, before whom I stand, surely there shall be neither dew nor rain these years, except by my word' " (1 Kings
17:1). His next public appearance is on Mount Carmel three
and a half years later, after the land is thoroughly parched
due to lack of rain. The dry conditions in Israel reflect the
spiritual barrenness of the people. Following the lead of
their king, Ahab, and his pagan queen, Jezebel, the Israelites
have turned away from God to worship Baal, the fertility god
of the Canaanites. Idolatry rules the land.

From the summit of Mount Carmel Elijah casts down a
challenge to his countrymen: "How long will you hesitate
between two opinions? If the Lord is God, follow Him; but if
Baal, follow him" (1 Kings 18:21b). These words are a prelude to the great contest between Elijah and the 450
prophets of Baal. Both sides prepare a sacrifice. Hours of
praying and wailing by Baal's prophets bring no response
from their god. Elijah then prays a simple prayer to the God
of Israel: "O Lord, the God of Abraham, Isaac and Israel,
today let it be known that Thou art God in Israel, and that I
am Thy servant, and that I have done all these things at Thy
word. Answer me, O Lord, answer me, that this people may
know that Thou, O Lord, art God, and that *Thou hast turned
their heart back again*" (1 Kings 18:36b-37).

Immediately, fire falls from Heaven and consumes the
sacrifice, the altar, and even the water with which they had
been drenched. In the face of this display of divine power,
the people proclaim their faith in the Lord and at Elijah's
direction kill all the prophets of Baal. This event marks the
end of the drought.

On the heels of this victory, Elijah flees for his life
because of Jezebel's vow to kill him. He undergoes a 40-day
fast in the wilderness and ends up on Mount Horeb, the
mountain of God, where the Lord speaks to him in a "still
small voice" (1 Kings 19:12b KJV). Assuring Elijah that there

are 7,000 people in Israel who have never bowed to Baal, God then instructs the prophet to anoint Elisha as his prophetic successor and Jehu as king of Israel. Elisha, who will carry a double portion of Elijah's anointing, represents the next generation of those who are radically committed to God. Jehu's destiny will be to destroy the house of Ahab, destroy Jezebel, and remove their gross idolatry from the land. The time of compromise and submission to godless rule is over.

Elijah's passion for God sparked a spiritual revolution in Israel that ignited on Mount Carmel and blazed all the way to Mount Horeb, giving birth to a whole new generation of prophets and transforming even the political arena of the nation.

ENOUGH IS ENOUGH!

A similar situation exists in America today. For four decades the Body of Christ has watched—mostly in silence—as the voice of the Church and the laws of God have been progressively legislated out of the public arena. Humanism, hedonism, and rationalism rule in the land as Americans worship at the altars of greed, materialism, and selfishness. Although founded and established on solid biblical principles of faith and law, the United States has turned away from these time-tested truths to follow other gods. Consider these signs of the nation's progressive decline:

- *Engle v. Vitale*, 1962, the New York court case that removed prayer from the public schools of America.

- *Roe v. Wade*, 1973, the Texas court case that legalized abortion on demand, giving the U.S. the most liberalized abortion standards in the world.

- *Stone v. Graham*, 1980, the Kentucky court case that declared as unconstitutional the posting of the Ten Commandments in the nation's schools and other public buildings.

- Increasingly lenient standards regarding "acceptable" language, violence, and sexual content in movies, television, music, books, and magazines.

- Significant decline in overall educational standards and quality.

- Sharp increase in divorce, violent crime, suicides, and teenage/unwed pregnancies.

- Erosion of the traditional nuclear family.

The Body of Christ in America stands at a "Mount Carmel moment" in time. A latter-day "Elijah's Revolution" is underway where a whole generation of believers is rising up like Elijah of old to proclaim, "Enough is enough!" There is no more hiding, no more silence, no more compromise, no more quiet acquiescence while the forces of sin and darkness continue to advance in the land.

These radical revolutionaries are sick to death of empty religion and the exaltation of human flesh. Hungry for holiness and for the Lord alone, they cry for the God of Elijah to arise and the fire from Heaven to fall. This is a whole new breed of believers who live not for the professional robes of religion but for the camel's hair of self-denial and sacrifice.

All over the country, young believers and older alike are answering the call to a revolution not of violence and destruction, but of love, prayer, consecration, and radical devotion to Christ. It is the revolution of a new generation rising up to confront and destroy false ideologies through prayer and fasting. It is the revolution of a new generation who refuse to give themselves to the lusts of the world, choosing instead to separate themselves in holy bridal devotion to Jesus Christ. It is the revolution of a new generation who willingly offer themselves as living sacrifices, holy and acceptable to the Lord (see Rom. 12:1).

In this day God is looking for a "flash point" for revival, a few anointed vessels upon whom He can send His fire. He is seeking a "revival core" of radical believers who will burn with the same passion for Christ as did the early Church; believers who will pray, "Let us be the altar upon whom Your fire falls." This is true intercession, where the people praying become the answer and the embodiment of their own prayer. They are so consumed with the desire for God's glory to fill the earth and transform the nations that they say, "I will be the altar and the sacrifice; only let Your fire fall!"

Prophetic intercessors find out what God wants to do now, and then set themselves to birth it through fasting and prayer. The need of the hour demands nothing less.

THIS IS YOUR TIME

Martyrdom has always been a flash point for the growth of the Church. Tertullian, an early Church father of the third century, said, "The blood of the martyrs is the seed of the Church." This is borne out both in Scripture and in history. In Elijah's day, the incident that sparked the beginning of the end for Ahab and Jezebel was the murder of Naboth, an innocent and righteous man, simply because he refused to sell his vineyard to the king. The martyrdom of Stephen in the seventh chapter of Acts set off a great persecution of the church in Jerusalem that also had the effect of scattering those early believers to other parts of the Roman Empire where they proceeded to transform their world through the message and power of the gospel. It has always been during times of persecution and martyrdom that the Church has shown its greatest and strongest growth.

Columbine was an earthquake in the spirit, and its after-shocks are still being felt nationwide, particularly in the Church and especially among young people. Satan overplayed his hand at Columbine. On April 20, 1999, when martyrs like Cassie Bernall and Rachel Scott, knowing they were about to die, looked their killers in the eye and said, "Yes, I believe in God," something shook loose in the nation and the stirrings of revival began. Columbine was the catalyst, the flash point that ignited the "Elijah Revolution" that is now sweeping the land. A new boldness has returned to the Church and many believers are now rising up to say, "We will not be cowed anymore. No matter how long it takes, no matter the cost, we will stand for Christ and for the turning of our nation back to God."

The martyrs of Columbine took a stand and entered the company of those who "overcame...because of the blood of the Lamb and because of the word of their testimony, and they did not love their life even to death" (Rev. 12:11). Inspired by their courage, Christian artists and songwriters Michael W. Smith and Wes King penned a song that should serve as a challenge to every believer today.

THIS IS YOUR TIME

It was a test we could all hope to pass
But none of us would want to take
Faced with the choice to deny God and live
For her there was one choice to make

This was her time
This was her dance
She lived every moment
Left nothing to chance
She swam in the sea
Drank of the deep
Embraced the mystery of all she could be
This was her time

Though you are mourning, and grieving your loss
Death died a long time ago
Swallowed in life, so her life carries on
Still, it's so hard to let go

This was her time
This was her dance
She lived every moment
Left nothing to chance
She swam in the sea
Drank of the deep
Embraced the mystery of all she could be
What if tomorrow, What if today
Faced with the question
Oh, what would you say

This is your time
This is your dance
Live every moment
Leave nothing to chance
Swim in the sea
Drink of the deep,
And fall on the mercy
And hear yourself praying
Won't you save me[5]

The need is urgent and the call has gone out. It is time for a holy revolution of love, grace, and forgiveness to stand resolutely casting the bright light of Christ over the darkness in the land. How will *you* respond? Will you answer the call? Are you ready to submit yourself to God as a living and holy sacrifice acceptable to Him, and to be the altar upon whom His fire can fall? Does your heart burn with passion for Christ and a yearning to see a great awakening in the land? The hour has come! This is your time!

ENDNOTES

1. Although the general name "America" properly includes all nations and peoples of North, Central, and South Americas, its use in this book, without any geographic qualifier, is to be understood as referring specifically to the United States.

2. Dr. Ché H. Ahn and Lou Engle, *The Call Revolution* (Colorado Springs, CO: Wagner Publications, 2001), p. 17.

3. The primary biblical reference to Nazirites is the sixth chapter of Numbers, which describes in detail the specific instructions and conditions regarding the Nazirite vow. The most familiar Nazirites in the Bible are Samson, Samuel, and John the Baptist. More information on Nazirites, especially the new generation of them who are arising in the Church today, is found in Chapter Four.

4. See Mt. 11:7-14; 17:11-13; Lk. 1:13-17.

5. © 1999 Milene Music, Inc. / Deer Valley Music (Admin by Milene Music, Inc) / ASCAP / Sparrow Song / Uncle Ivan Music / (Both Admin by EMI Christian Music Publishing) / BMI).

Chapter Two

...For a New Prophetic Generation

One of the heart cries of this modern band of holy revolutionaries is for God's glory to fill the earth. Their passionate prayer is that the transcendent majesty of Christ would permeate His people as He is lifted up for all the nations to behold. With keen anticipation they call on the Lord to visit His house again.

God has deposited a dream that has grabbed hold of their hearts and permanently ruined them for "Christianity as usual." Energized by the truth that God is the same yesterday, today, and forever (see Heb. 13:8), they look to Him to move in the midst of His people in this generation as He did in generations past. Their spirits burn with a vision of Jesus Christ in all His glory. No longer content simply to live by the rules of "do's and don'ts," they so yearn to be close to Him that they freely cast away anything and everything in their lives that keep them from His presence, and abandon themselves completely to Him. They have caught a glimpse of glory, their spiritual eyes forever seared by the brilliance of the transcendent majesty of Christ.

THE TRANSCENDENT MAJESTY OF CHRIST

No one who sees such a vision of the glorious Christ can ever look at Him or at life in quite the same way afterward. It has a way of changing one's perspective. Jim Goll can vouch for this, because he had just such an encounter at a prayer conference some time ago.

> The whole time I was there I had tried to be *incognito*, but on Saturday night the prophetic warfare mantle on the worship was so strong that I just couldn't handle it any longer. Toward the end I went forward and stood right in front of the blaring speakers. As the sounds washed over me in waves I was saying, "More, Lord, just blast me." At that moment I forgot about this life and about this world. I forgot about who I was, who I thought I was supposed to be, and even who other people thought I was supposed to be. I forgot about dignity and reputation and simply stood there weeping as the Holy Spirit "blasted" me.
>
> Suddenly I saw a white horse march forth. On the stirrup leather down the side of its saddle was written the word "Holiness." Then I saw another word, "Holy War." At the same time I saw the Lord as a warrior stepping forward and mounting His war horse. I realized that He was preparing to make an announcement. His holy war was coming. But this is not a battle of one man fighting another, but rather the battle of the ages of the Kingdom of Light against the kingdom of darkness.

After this I saw clouds, and stairs in the clouds. They reminded me of the old rock and roll song "Stairway to Heaven." In my vision I was walking up these stairs one step at a time. As I rose higher and higher I began to see bright white light until finally, on a platform at the top, I was surrounded by it. All around me was nothing but brilliant, white shining light that shot through me from side to side and up and down, illuminating everything inside of me and transfusing every fiber of my being. It was incredibly beautiful. The brilliance of His great presence permeated me as I wept uncontrollably. Caught up in this vision of the transcendent majesty of Christ, I stood transfixed until finally I began to cry out loud, "Oh Lord, You're beautiful, You're beautiful, You're beautiful."

I don't know how long I cried and don't care, because this vision gave me another taste, another picture, of the Lord. It deposited in me a desire to see His transcendent majesty permeate all of us. I want to see the light of God penetrate us and drive out the darkness. I want to see the holiness of God fill His Church. I want to see the Body of Christ become overwhelmed with the loveliness of His great presence.

THE GOD OF MORE THAN ENOUGH

All over the country radical revolutionaries are rising up who hunger and thirst for the righteousness of God and for the waves and billows of His brilliant presence to wash over them like a flood. They are so overcome by His love and beauty that they want nothing else but to give themselves in holy abandonment to the purposes of God in their generation.

While they long for the presence of God, they are sick to death of "religion" with its unholy and worldly spirit that squelches vision, locks people into puny mind-sets of small thinking, and tries to confine God in a tiny box of human design. Instead, their heart's desire is to see the God who is more than enough; the God who is able to take those who *cannot* and transform them into those who *can*. Like most revolutionaries, they are visionaries and dreamers, the vanguard of a new prophetic generation.

Dreams and visions are a significant part of God's supernatural prophetic presence with His people today just as they have been in ages past. One purpose of the prophetic is to break the Body of Christ out of limited "religious" mind-sets into the world of the supernatural, the world of the God who is "I am that I am" and of Jesus Christ who is the same yesterday, today, and forever. In this hour God is birthing a new refined prophetic faith message in the hearts of His children. To a people who *cannot*, He is saying, "I will do it through you. I am the God of breakthrough, the God of change. I am El Shaddai, the Almighty; I am Jehovah Jireh, your Provider. I will make a way where there is no way. Step out in obedience into that which you know not of, and watch what I will do."

The prophetic anointing, including dreams and visions, is one way God creates faith in the hearts of His people so they will walk in obedience and, through prayer and fasting, help give birth to God's purposes in the earth. This new prophetic generation follows in the footsteps and precedent of centuries of prophetic people, going all the way back to Abraham.

ABRAHAM THE DREAMER

Abraham is the first person the Bible specifically calls a prophet (see Gen. 20:7). The Books of Galatians and Romans both refer to Abraham as the father of the faithful. He was the physical ancestor of the nation of Israel, yet could not bring forth in the natural because his wife, Sarah, was barren. Abram and Sarai (their original names) had no children and eventually grew old and beyond child-bearing age. God, however, had given Abram a vision—a dream that he would be the father of an entire nation. That dream sustained and carried Abram until he saw it super-naturally fulfilled.

From the beginning of his walk with God, Abram was a dreamer and a visionary, willing to move on nothing more than a word from the Lord.

> *Now the Lord said to Abram, "Go forth from your coun-try, and from your relatives and from your father's house, to the land which I will show you; and I will make you a great nation, and I will bless you, and make your name great; and so you shall be a blessing; and I will bless those who bless you, and the one who curses you I will curse. And in you all the families of the earth shall be blessed." So Abram went forth as the Lord had spoken to him; and Lot went with him. Now Abram was seventy-five years old when he departed from Haran. And Abram took Sarai his wife and Lot his nephew, and all their possessions which they had accumulated, and the persons which they had acquired in Haran, and they set out for the land of Canaan; thus they came to the land of Canaan (Genesis 12:1-5).*

Some time after Abram settled in Canaan with his family, the Lord visited him again with word of an awesome promise.

> *After these things the word of the Lord came to Abram in a vision, saying, "Do not fear, Abram, I am a shield to you; your reward shall be very great." And Abram said, "O Lord God, what wilt Thou give me, since I am child-less, and the heir of my house is Eliezer of Damascus?"*

And Abram said, "Since Thou hast given no offspring to
me, one born in my house is my heir." Then behold, the
word of the Lord came to him, saying, "This man will not
be your heir; but one who shall come forth from your own
body, he shall be your heir." And He took him outside and
said, "Now look toward the heavens, and count the stars,
if you are able to count them." And He said to him, "So
shall your descendants be." Then he believed in the Lord;
and He reckoned it to him as righteousness (Genesis
15:1-6).

Verse 6 of this passage states matter-of-factly that Abram
"believed in the Lord," but consider the depth of his faith:
He who was too old to have children would yet father a son
in his old age. Moreover, through that son Abram would
become the "father" of a multitude as countless as the stars.
Abram walked the rest of his days with this divine vision of his
fruitfulness in front of him.

The significance to Abram of this prophetic promise
from the Lord is seen even in his name change.

Now when Abram was ninety-nine years old, the Lord
appeared to Abram and said to him, "I am God Almighty;
walk before Me, and be blameless. And I will establish My
covenant between Me and you, and I will multiply you
exceedingly." And Abram fell on his face, and God talked
with him, saying, "As for Me, behold, My covenant is
with you, and you shall be the father of a multitude of
nations. No longer shall your name be called Abram, but
your name shall be Abraham; for I will make you the
father of a multitude of nations. And I will make you
exceedingly fruitful, and I will make nations of you, and
kings shall come forth from you" (Genesis 17:1-6).

"Abram" means "exalted father" (an ironic name for a
childless man), while "Abraham" means "father of a multitude." Through the power of God's Word which could not

fail, Abram, the man who could not, was transformed into Abraham, the man who could. Abraham and Sarah brought forth Isaac, whose name means "laughter." The old man and his barren wife laughed and laughed because they who could not were enabled by the God who is more than enough. For the rest of their lives, whenever they went outside at night the stars spoke to them, calling out for the numberless descendants of Abraham to come forth.

Centuries later, a new generation has arisen, a generation of faith, a generation of spiritual descendants of Abraham whom God wants to enable by pouring into them the same prophetic presence that was in their forefather.

PROPHETIC BIRTH AND DELIVERANCE

The Church in this hour is entering a new dimension. Christ is preparing His Body to receive the coming waves of God's glory. A new age of birth and deliverance is at hand that is in the same spirit as those who have gone before. Throughout the Word of God, the cycle of birth and deliverance is a recurring theme that defines and illustrates the process by which God relates to people.

For example, when God wanted to raise up a people for Himself He called Abraham. Through his son Isaac and his descendants, Abraham birthed the nation of Israel. Several generations later, Abraham's progeny had grown to a great multitude who toiled and suffered under the yoke of slavery in Egypt. The children of Israel needed a deliverer.

When God's time was right, Moses appeared on the scene. Moses represented the arrival of a special prophetic generation promising the deliverance of God's people. Much work had to be done as a forerunner of that deliverance. God spent 80 years preparing Moses for his appointed role as deliverer. Forty years in the courts of pharaoh and another 40 years in the deserts of Midian shaped and molded Moses' character for the mission that lay ahead. Coupled with this was God's supernatural empowerment, which enabled Moses to accomplish God's purpose of leading the nation of Israel to freedom.

It was a prophetic generation filled with signs and wonders: water turned to blood; plagues of frogs, gnats, flies, cattle-killing disease, boils, hail, and locusts; darkness that covered the land for three days; and finally, the deaths of all the first-born of the Egyptians. The signs and wonders continued after the exodus as well: the parting of the waters at the Red Sea, water from the rock in the wilderness, daily manna from heaven, and the pillar of cloud by day and pillar of fire by night. Moses' deliverance of the Hebrews from Egyptian slavery gave birth to the state of Israel.

But anything God seeks to birth satan tries to destroy. The enemy has partial knowledge. He can see in part and knew a deliverer was due, but he did not know exactly when or where. By moving the Egyptian pharaoh to decree that all male Hebrew babies were to be killed (see Ex. 1:15-17), satan attempted to prevent God's chosen deliverer from reaching manhood. Whenever God pronounces a day of deliverance, satan hatches a plot to take out the deliverer.

Hundreds of years later another day of deliverance was at hand, a day announced ahead of time by generations of God's prophets. The Father sent His only Son to be born of a virgin, to walk the earth as a man, to die a criminal's death on a cross as the Lamb of God who takes away the sin of the world, and to rise from the dead as the firstfruit and guarantee of eternal life for all who believed. A forerunner, John the Baptist, came to prepare the way for the coming of the Messiah. John was the "Elijah" of his generation and turned the hearts of many children and fathers back to the Lord. Then Jesus Christ Himself appeared, and by His death and resurrection birthed redemption for all mankind and brought deliverance from sin and death.

Once again the enemy attempted to destroy God's chosen deliverer by inciting Herod to order the killing of all male children two years old and under in the region around Jerusalem and Bethlehem. God protected His Son. Using dreams and visions, God spoke to the wise men about not returning to Herod. He also warned Joseph to flee to Egypt with Mary and Jesus and, after Herod died, led them to return and settle in Galilee (see Mt. 2).

John the Baptist personified a chosen prophetic generation in the spirit of Elijah who arose to prepare the way for the Messiah's first coming. In the same way, according to the Scriptures, a prophetic "Elijah" generation will arise also in the last days to prepare the way for His second coming. It will be a "faceless" generation in the sense that there will be not only highly visible leaders or "point" people who have incredible encounters with God. God also will place His prophetic presence on an entire generation, and they will walk in holiness and absolute surrender to Him, enjoying face-to-face intimacy with Him to an unprecedented degree. Yes, an entire generation of radical warriors shall arise!

This prophetic generation will not be interested in recognition, reputation, or in making a name for themselves. Their only concern will be the glory of the Lord in the earth. Through prayer and fasting they will birth spiritual awakening and revival on a global scale that will bring deliverance to people in every land.

As always, satan will attempt to prevent this from happening. He has already been busy for years. Abortion, alcohol and drug abuse, violent crime, and deterioration of moral standards and the traditional family are only a few of the enemy's weapons in his all-out crusade to destroy this generation before they can fulfill their God-ordained destiny.

But God's purpose will not be thwarted! His plan will not fail. All that God has ordained He will bring to pass.

A Scepter From Zion

The Bible is filled with prophetic references to the coming of Christ. Prophecies of Christ's coming are not confined only to the books of prophecy; a surprising number are found in the Psalms. As with prophetic references found elsewhere, messianic prophecies in the Psalms fall generally into two categories: those that relate primarily to Christ's first coming, and those that refer mainly to His second coming. Looking through the lens of history and divine revelation it is possible to see in these Psalms clear parallels in the life of Jesus.

Psalm 110 is a messianic psalm that relates to the second coming of Christ. This is clear in both the wording and the circumstances described:

> *The Lord says to my Lord: "Sit at My right hand until I make Thine enemies a footstool for Thy feet." The Lord will stretch forth Thy strong scepter from Zion, saying, "Rule in the midst of Thine enemies." Thy people will volunteer freely in the day of Thy power; in holy array, from the womb of the dawn, Thy youth are to Thee as the dew. The Lord has sworn and will not change His mind, "Thou art a priest forever according to the order of Melchizedek." The Lord is at Thy right hand; He will shatter kings in the day of His wrath. He will judge among the nations, He will fill them with corpses, He will shatter the chief men over a broad country. He will drink from the brook by the wayside; therefore He will lift up His head (Psalm 110).*

This psalm is structured as if God the Father is speaking to His Son while David, the psalmist, observes and narrates.

Verse 2 says that the Messiah's "strong scepter" will "stretch forth" from "Zion." In the Scriptures, the word *Zion* is used in several different ways. One of its most common meanings is in reference to the city of God in the messianic age. It is the heavenly Jerusalem where the Messiah will appear at the end of time and where His people will be glorified. *Zion* also can refer to the whole assembly of God's people—the believing Jews of the old covenant as well as the Body of Christ of the new covenant—among whom He lives and works.

From this perspective, this psalm pictures a coming day when a transference of authority will be given by God to Zion—His covenant people—through Yeshua (Jesus) the Messiah, and they will rule with Him even in the midst of enemies. In that future "day of [the Messiah's] power" His people will "volunteer freely...in holy array." A great host of believers will willingly abandon themselves to their Lord and walk in holiness and consecration to carry out His will and accomplish His purpose.

As that day approaches the dark will get darker but the light will get brighter. It will be a time both of great glory and great judgment upon the nations. The Lord will "shatter kings in the day of His wrath" and "chief men over a broad country." He will "fill [the nations] with corpses." It will be a time of great tension. It will be a time of great darkness and a time of great light; a time of great judgment and a time of great hope; a time of great wrath and a time of great revival; a time of great destruction and a time of great restoration.

Things are going to get worse, but they also will get better. Those who have their faith fixed on the Lord shall be changed from glory to glory. They will be bright and shining lights in the midst of the darkness, and many will be drawn to their brightness.

RESTORING RADICAL CHRISTIANITY

P salm 102 is another messianic psalm related to the return of Christ. Consider these verses from the middle of the psalm:

But Thou, O Lord, dost abide forever; and Thy name to all generations. Thou wilt arise and have compassion on Zion; for it is time to be gracious to her, for the appointed time has come. Surely Thy servants find pleasure in her stones, and feel pity for her dust. So the nations will fear the name of the Lord, and all the kings of the earth Thy glory. For the Lord has built up Zion; He has appeared in His glory. He has regarded the prayer of the destitute, nor has He despised their prayer. This will be written for the generation to come; that a people yet to be created may praise the Lord (Psalm 102:12-18).

This passage speaks of an "appointed time" when "the nations will fear the name of the Lord, and all the kings of the earth Thy glory." Although such a day has not yet arrived, there are many signs that suggest it may be near. The gospel of Jesus Christ has begun to spread into many nations and regions of the world formerly closed to it. Response to the gospel, particularly in non-Western parts of the world, is growing at a rate unprecedented in history since the first century.

Another indicator that a new chosen prophetic generation may be at hand is that there is now underway in the world the greatest prayer movement ever in the history of the Church. Surveys indicate that as many as 170 million believers worldwide pray daily for spiritual awakening and for the revival of the Church. There are 10 million prayer groups around the world that pray for revival every week.

This is absolutely unprecedented in Church history. It is unprecedented in breadth because it is not confined to one nation. It is unprecedented in scope because it is not limited to one denomination. It is unprecedented in strategy because it is a wedding of prayer and evangelism. Prayer has always been one of the greatest weapons of the Church, particularly before and during times of awakening and revival. It is no different today. From the beginning of the current "Elijah Revolution," prayer, and especially intercession, has been the foremost strategy of this generation of holy warriors that God is calling forth.

Coupled with this call to sacrificial prayer and intercession is a call to fasting that is more widespread than ever before in the Body of Christ. After generations of neglect, fasting as a powerful spiritual discipline is being rediscovered across a broad spectrum of the Church. Over 200 years ago John Wesley, the fiery preacher, evangelist, and founder of Methodism, would not ordain anyone to the ministry unless he was committed to fasting two days a week. Wesley's fire is being restored to the Church. In this new chosen prophetic generation fasting will no longer be thought of as a sign of extreme or "abnormal" Christianity, but as an integral part of life in the Spirit.

"Normal" Christianity has *always* been "extreme": extreme devotion to the person of Jesus Christ; extreme abandonment of self-will and absolute surrender to the will and purposes of God; extreme love for God that totally consumes one's heart, soul, mind, and strength. "Elijah's Revolution" represents nothing less than the restoration of raw, radical Christianity in this generation—Christianity as it is *supposed* to be!

PREPARING THE WAY FOR CHRIST'S COMING

The Book of Joel prophesied that a chosen prophetic generation would arise on the earth before the great and terrible day of the Lord, a whole generation of dreamers and visionaries who would move in signs and wonders.

> *And it will come about after this that I will pour out My Spirit on all mankind; and your sons and daughters will prophesy, your old men will dream dreams, your young men will see visions. And even on the male and female servants I will pour out My Spirit in those days. And I will display wonders in the sky and on the earth, blood, fire, and columns of smoke. The sun will be turned into darkness, and the moon into blood, before the great and awesome day of the Lord comes. And it will come about that whoever calls on the name of the Lord will be delivered; for on Mount Zion and in Jerusalem there will be those who escape, as the Lord has said, even among the survivors whom the Lord calls* (Joel 2:28-32).

A tidal wave of God's glory is breaking over the Body of Christ. The swell has been rising for years. Fresh revelations of the grace and mercy of God have given birth to an unparalleled movement of intercessory prayer that continues to grow. A greater release of the spiritual giftings of God upon His people is leading to a fuller restoration of His manifest presence and power in the midst of His Church. In the new prophetic generation signs and wonders will not be limited to a select few or a handful of "point" people, but will manifest more broadly throughout the Body of believers.

That is the prophetic destiny of this generation. God's tidal wave of glory will break through the "brass bowl" that has covered the earth. The curse will be lifted, the heavens will be opened once again, the "day of the Lord's power" will be revealed, and He will appear in His glory in Zion. God has chosen a new generation to place His prophetic presence upon as a forerunner to prepare for Christ's appearance in glory.

This forerunner generation will be the vanguard of a global awakening unlike any other in history. The time is coming when the South American anointing will be wedded with the North American anointing in Jesus' name. Strategies of the North will be joined with the raw power of the South, and a new deliverance movement will arise. The graces of the East and the West shall merge together as well as the thrust's calling forth sacrificial prayer for the 10/40 and now the 40/70 prayer window emerge.

Even now a window of divine deliverance is opening. It is global in nature. The call is being released. Do you hear it? Passion and power through the name of Jesus is leading to the breaking of curses, soul ties, and wrong emotional affections of the past, and deliverance from the spirits of insanity, unclean spirits, and idolatry. As He did in the Temple so long ago, Jesus is invading His Church in order to clean house for His name's sake. A new prophetic generation is being born. The spiritual destiny of the Church is being restored to the land.

The prophetic helps prepare the way for the purposes of God in a generation and ultimately for Christ's coming. According to the Book of Acts, Jesus will not return until the fullness of time has come and all the prophecies of old have been fulfilled.

> *Repent therefore and return, that your sins may be wiped away, in order that times of refreshing may come from the presence of the Lord; and that He may send Jesus, the Christ appointed for you, whom heaven must receive until the period of restoration of all things about which God spoke by the mouth of His holy prophets from ancient time* (Acts 3:19-21).

God raises up a prophetic generation for the purpose of praying the prophetic promises of old into being. The prophetic opens the door to restoration, which paves the way for the coming of Christ. In this way, a prophetic generation helps the Church as a whole prepare to be the Bride of Christ.

Will this generation witness the second coming of Christ? Only God the Father knows. He alone will determine whether the appearance of Christ in glory among His people in this day is a historic renewal of His manifest presence or the literal, visible return where He splits the eastern sky. Either way, the Father is pouring out His prophetic anointing like fragrant oil over the Bride of Christ in order to prepare her for the coming of the Bridegroom.

The Lord is mounting His holy war horse, and He is releasing a call. Will you ride with Him and be a part of His purposes for a new prophetic generation?

Chapter Three

...For the Joining of the Generations

If the Church hopes to be relevant and meet the needs of the twenty-first century and beyond, it must be willing to undergo a paradigm shift. The Elijah Revolution confronts the status quo by challenging the Church to reexamine many of its assumptions. One of these assumptions is what could be called the "quick escape mentality."

For over a century many believers have been taught that the endtimes are near and to expect Christ to take His Church at any moment. This teaching has been especially prevalent in the evangelical branch of the Church. Whether or not this interpretation of prophecy is accurate is not the point. What is important is the influence it has had on the mind-set of the Church. One positive result of the "rapture mentality" is that it has created in many Christians a sense of urgency with regard to evangelism and missions. If Christ could return "any day," then there is no time to lose in telling others about Him. On the other hand, this same mentality can have the unfortunate consequence of discouraging long-term thinking. If everything is about to come to an end anyway, why focus on the future?

Jim Goll recalls how this short-term mind-set plagued him in his early years of the Jesus People Movement. Zeal was abounding and the Holy Spirit was moving across the university he was attending. He became a Jesus Person and lived with other young men in a Jesus House. He thought he knew that Jesus was returning any moment to come and get His people out of this messy world.

A couple of the other young leaders planted a small rosebud tree in the front yard of the Jesus House. Jim admits today that when he saw this he became disturbed and stated to the others, "What are you doing spending money to plant that tree? Don't you know that Jesus will return long before that tree ever grows into maturity!"

Time passed; the tree grew. It became a beautiful flowering reminder to Jim (and others) that maybe God had a long-timer's mind-set for the fullness of His purposes to come to pass. Time has changed. Today Jim and Lou (and hopefully you) think "generationally."

THINKING GENERATIONALLY

The modern Church must rediscover the mind-set of thinking *generationally*. There are at least two reasons for this. First, no one but the Father knows when Jesus will return—it could be today, tomorrow, or many years from now—and second, God Himself always thinks and acts generationally. For too long too many members of the Body of Christ have considered themselves part of a terminal generation. It is time to change that way of thinking. Each generation of Christians needs to see itself as a bridge generation that builds on the past, lives in the present, and plans for the future. It is important to live each day as if Christ is coming back today, yet plan for tomorrow as if He will not return for years.

Part of the mind-set of a bridge generation is recognizing and taking seriously the responsibility of passing on to the next generation a solid legacy of faith and godly values. Just how important is this "generational transfer"? Long ago someone observed that the Church is never more than one generation away from paganism. All it takes to lose everything is for one generation to fail in transferring its beliefs and principles to the next.

There are disturbing signs that this has been happening in America for years. A recent study released by the Barna Research Group, a Christian organization highly respected for its accurate tracking of trends in contemporary religious thought, revealed that among adult members of America's 12 largest denominations, only 41 percent could be classified as "born again." Of all the adults surveyed, 41 percent believed that the Bible was completely accurate. Only 40 percent believed that Jesus Christ lived a sinless life, while, incredibly, only 27 percent believed satan was a real being.[1] Remember, these are not unchurched people; these are *church members* and *professing Christians*! If this is what the "middle" generation believes, is it any wonder that so many of the "younger" generation have no spiritual anchor in their lives?

One of the most critical needs of the Church today is to renew its commitment to "generational transfer": passing on to the next generation not just principles, theology, and doctrinal beliefs, but also passionate *heart affection*. Each generation must learn to love God for themselves, and it is the responsibility of the preceding generation to teach them by modeling that love. This is the biblical pattern, not only in God's dealings with man, but also in the patriarchs' dealings with their children. It is a fundamental principle known as mentoring—*spiritual fathering and mothering*.

SPIRITUAL MENTORING

The principles of both spiritual mentoring and generational transfer are firmly grounded in Scripture.

For the ancient Israelites they were foundational concepts of the Mosaic Law. One of the best examples is found in the sixth chapter of Deuteronomy.

> *Hear, O Israel! The Lord is our God, the Lord is one! And you shall love the Lord your God with all your heart and with all your soul and with all your might. And these words, which I am commanding you today, shall be on your heart; and you shall teach them diligently to your sons and shall talk of them when you sit in your house and when you walk by the way and when you lie down and when you rise up.... When your son asks you in time to come, saying, "What do the testimonies and the statutes and the judgments mean which the Lord commanded you?" then you shall say to your son, "We were slaves to Pharaoh in Egypt; and the Lord brought us from Egypt with a mighty hand. Moreover, the Lord showed great and distressing signs and wonders before our eyes against Egypt, Pharaoh and all his household; and He brought us out from there in order to bring us in, to give us the land which He had sworn to our fathers." So the Lord commanded us to observe all these statutes, to fear the Lord our God for our good always and for our survival, as it is today. And it will be righteousness for us if we are careful to observe all this commandment before the Lord our God, just as He commanded us* (Deuteronomy 6:4-7,20-25).

Verses 4 and 5 constitute what is known as the *shema* (from the first word of the passage in Hebrew), which devout Jews regard as the foundational truth for their faith. The *shema* is also the first Scripture that Jewish children are taught as they begin their spiritual education: "Hear, O Israel! The Lord is our God, the Lord is one! And you shall love the Lord your God with all your heart and with all your soul and with all your might." In Matthew 22:38 Jesus identified this as the "great and foremost commandment." Nothing is of greater importance than knowing, loving, and fearing God.

On the heels of the commandment to love God is the command to pass on that love, as well as the knowledge and love of all God's law, to the next generation. "These words, which I am commanding you today, shall be on your heart; and you shall teach them diligently to your sons and shall talk of them when you sit in your house and when you walk by the way and when you lie down and when you rise up." The fathers (and mothers) were to use every walk and circumstance of life as an opportunity to transfer the legacy of faith to their children.

Generational transfer does not happen overnight. There are no shortcuts, no pat formulas, or "25-words-or-less" summary statements for imparting faith and values. There are no *Cliff's Notes®* for a crash course in spiritual mentoring. (There is no manual called *Spiritual Multiplication for Dummies.*) Success comes only with commitment, discipline, diligence, and patience. These qualities are fast becoming quaint notions of the past in today's fast-paced "microwave" society of instant gratification and ten-second sound bites.

This same attitude has become quite common throughout much of the Body of Christ. Many believers are spiritually impatient, preferring the quick touch of the Lord and the hot blaze of revival to the slower and less dramatic but more demanding pace of discipline and mentoring. In truth, the fast burn of revival and the slow burn of spiritual mentoring are both critical to God's strategy for reaching the nations. Revival releases faith and changes individual lives while spiritual mentoring transforms culture.

The fire of God that fell on Mount Carmel was the fast burn of revival. It released faith in the hearts of the Israelites that God was greater than Baal, but it did not turn the nation. Ahab and Jezebel still remained in power. At the same time, a switch began to occur. The Mount Carmel revival also ignited a slow-burning flame that stirred an underground movement of spiritual revolution that climaxed many years later in cultural transformation.

God led Elijah from Mount Carmel to Mount Horeb—from the fire to the fast—and told the prophet to anoint Elisha as his successor. The "still, small voice" of God said to Elijah, "Go and give yourself to a spiritual son." Elijah became a spiritual father to Elisha. The next time Elijah appears is toward the end of his life when he is calling down fire to consume the soldiers of the king. He is literally shaking the nation. Elijah has mentored Elisha, his spiritual son, as well as other spiritual sons in every city, and the slow burn of revolution is taking over. That is how nations and cultures are transformed.

Elijah set the stage by his faithfulness as a spiritual father, but it is the next generation under Elisha and Jehu that destroys Jezebel, who represents the domination of culture by the powers of darkness, and brings transformation to the land.

A SYNERGY OF GENERATIONS

*S*ynergy is defined as the condition where distinct groups work together in a cooperative arrangement in such a way that the total effect is greater than the sum of the individual effects. In other words, the group accomplishes more working together than the individual members could achieve working independently.

One of the things that the Elijah Revolution represents is God's desire to link multiple generations into a synergistic relationship once again. The Church has long suffered from a "generation gap" where there is little genuine appreciation, understanding, or cooperation between the older, middle, and younger generations of believers. God wants to bring these generations back together—to infuse them with a common vision, a unified sense of purpose, and a recognition of their mutual interdependence. Three generations moving together toward a shared goal can accomplish more than the sum of what each generation could achieve separately. This synergy of the generations is something that God promised He would bring about in the last days. Jim refers to this as the "convergence of the ages."

A "convergence of the ages" will come upon us. The falling of Pentecostal fire, healing and deliverance crusades, the latter rain presence, the evangelical burden for the lost, the charismatic giftings, the zeal of the Jesus people movement, the credibility of the third wave, the revelation of the prophetic movement, and the relational networking of the apostolic reformation—all will swell into a tidal wave greater than the impact of the Reformation five hundred years ago and create what could be called the great revolution.[2]

Before Christ returns, God will release an explosion of His Holy Spirit that will shatter paradigms in people's minds and cause the whole Church to begin thinking generationally rather than selfishly. A whole generation will begin to give themselves to their "Elishas," to raise up "double portion" sons and daughters who will dominate their culture in the power of the Holy Spirit.

These latter-day "Elishas" will be a new breed. Lou Engle describes them this way:

> Who are these sons and daughters? They are the ones who know the love and affirmation of a father. They are not governed by their hormones, but governed by the commands of God. They are not propped up by some cheap, self-help, build-your-self-esteem plan, but have been baptized in confidence because they've heard the voice of a father saying, "You are my beloved son." And they rule as a father for their

father. They stand in the face of every intimidating Jezebel because they build their house on the rock of obedience to God's Word. Though the rains fall and the winds blow, the house will stand....Our generational God is the God of Abraham, Isaac, and Jacob, and now we are receiving the synergy of the generations. A ruling generation is rising. Generational transfer and promotion is on the way.[3]

God is generational by nature. Even His self-revelation to humanity as Father, Son, and Holy Spirit—one God in three Persons—reflects a generational perspective. God the Father gave His only begotten Son to redeem lost humanity and make salvation possible for everyone who believes. God the Son gave Himself to a small band of spiritual sons and imparted to them the Holy Spirit to dwell within them continually. God the Holy Spirit empowers and enables believers to carry out the Father's redemptive plan on a global scale. Completion of the plan requires that all "generations" work together as one. Father, Son, and Holy Spirit are co-equal, co-existent, and co-eternal in nature but generational in relationship to mankind.

When God describes Himself as the God of Abraham, Isaac, and Jacob, He is not just identifying Himself by name; He is describing His very being and how His purposes proceed throughout history. God told Abraham that his children would be as the stars in the sky or the sand on the seashore, yet Abraham had only one son of promise: Isaac.[4] Isaac passed the promise on to his son, Jacob, who passed it on to his 12 sons, one of whom was Joseph, who rose to prominence in Egypt. After a small beginning, in the fourth generation one appeared who ruled an entire nation. All of Jacob's sons were fruitful, their descendants multiplying across many generations to become the 12 tribes of the nation of Israel.

SUCCESSION, NOT ORIGINALITY

Whenever there is a sustained, ongoing movement of God in revival, spiritual awakening, and Holy Spirit activity, multiple generations are always involved. God is the God of Abraham, Isaac, and Jacob. The congregation of God's people includes persons of all ages: "Gather the people, sanctify the congregation, assemble the elders, gather the children and the nursing infants. Let the bridegroom come out of his room and the bride out of her bridal chamber" (Joel 2:16). This call is a prelude to the great promise of verse 28, which is clearly transgenerational in nature: "It will come about after this that I will pour out My Spirit on all mankind; and your sons and daughters will prophesy, your old men will dream dreams, your young men will see visions." You could say it takes a young man's vision to fulfill an old man's dream!

In Malachi 4:5-6 the prophet speaks of "restor[ing] the hearts of the fathers to their children, and the hearts of the children to their fathers." The Elijah Revolution is one latter-day fulfillment of this promise, an embodiment of the "spirit of Elijah," which involves the joining of at least three generations. It is a synergistic, transgenerational anointing that links together the wisdom of the old, the resources of the middle, and the zeal of the young.

One of the major problems of Western culture that has also bled over into much of the modern Church is the placing of so much importance on independence and originality. God does not exalt originality; He exalts *succession*. The true heroes of the Bible and of Church history—the people who have accomplished the most for the Kingdom of God—are not those who went off on their own tangents, but those who patiently and faithfully carried on and built upon the work of their predecessors. This synergy between spiritual fathers (or mothers) and spiritual sons (or daughters) is the pattern of Scripture and a fundamental principle of how God works.

MULTIPLYING BY INVESTING

The prophet Elisha is a good example. He was not interested in being "original" but in being faithful to the spirit and prophetic mantle he inherited from Elijah, his spiritual father. As Lou Engle writes:

> Elisha did not seek to carve out his own ministry, but wore the mantle of this spiritual father as a badge of honor. He lived to fulfill the dreams of his dad. Because Elisha was willing to receive a father's heart, minister as a servant and son under that father, and submit to his discipline and training, he received the mantle and the double portion inheritance of Elijah's power and influence. He completed and multiplied Elijah's ministry and was used to turn the nation from Baal worship.[5]

Likewise, the apostles, the Gospel writers, and other early believers had no wish to be original or independent. Their only desire was to be true to Christ and to the gospel message, and faithful to the calling and commission He had given them. Luke made this clear at the very beginning of his writings: "Inasmuch as many have undertaken to compile an account of the things accomplished among us, *just as those* who from the beginning were eyewitnesses and servants of the Word have handed them down to us, it seemed fitting for me as well...*to write it out for you* in consecutive order" (Lk. 1:1-3a); and "*The first account I composed,* Theophilus, *about all that Jesus began to do and teach,* until the day when He was taken up, after He had by the Holy Spirit given orders to the apostles whom He had chosen" (Acts 1:1-2).

Paul was just as plain in his determination simply to pass on what the Lord gave to him: "But may it never be that I should boast, except in the cross of our Lord Jesus Christ..." (Gal. 6:14); "For I determined to know nothing among you except Jesus Christ, and Him crucified" (1 Cor. 2:2); "For *I delivered to you* as of first importance *what I also received...*" (1 Cor. 15:3); "For I received from the Lord that which I also delivered to you..." (1 Cor. 11:23).

These earliest Christians saw themselves merely as witnesses to and messengers of the truth revealed to them by the Lord. John the apostle began his first letter with these words: "What was from the beginning, *what we have heard, what we have seen with our eyes, what we beheld and our hands handled,* concerning the Word of Life...*what we have seen and heard we proclaim to you also,* that you also may have fellowship with us; and indeed our fellowship is with the Father, and with His Son Jesus Christ" (1 Jn. 1:1,3).

Even Jesus Himself was probably the most *unoriginal* man who ever lived. It could have been otherwise. Jesus could have been "original," but He chose instead to follow after His Father: "Truly, truly, I say to you, the Son can do nothing of Himself, unless it is something He sees the Father doing; for whatever the Father does, these things the Son also does in like manner....I can do nothing on My own initiative. As I hear, I judge; and My judgment is just, because I do not seek My own will, but the will of Him who sent Me" (Jn. 5:19b,30); "Do you not believe that I am in the Father, and the Father is in Me? The words that I say to you I do not speak on My own initiative, but the Father abiding in Me does His works" (Jn. 14:10). Like Elisha, Jesus "wore the mantle" of His Father as a badge of honor. Because Jesus was secure in His Father's love, He was secure saying and doing only that which came from His Father. Jesus was after succession, not originality.

RUNNING WITH THE VISION

God the Father delighted in His Son, but His whole being looked toward the day when He would send

His Son into the world. They were together in perfect harmony and fellowship from the beginning, but in the fullness of time, the Father released His Son to enter the human realm as a baby born of a virgin and laid in a manger. The child born became a Son given. As the Son matured in God, He learned obedience through the things that He suffered (see Heb. 5:8). Jesus Himself became a "father" as He multiplied Himself by gathering a band of spiritual "sons" and sending them out in His name: "Peace be with you; as the Father has sent Me, I also send you" (Jn. 20:21b).

This is God's plan for every person in every generation. God wants to do in each of us that which He did in His own Son. This is the process: A child born becomes through character testing the son (or daughter) given; these children given become parents who multiply themselves over and over and over again by raising up and nurturing spiritual sons and daughters. The parents pour their unconditional love into their children until they come to maturity, and then they release those children onto the stage of history.

The Father's great desire is to fill the earth with His spiritual children. This will happen not through a crash course in holiness, but through one generation patiently and faithfully passing on to the next not just information and knowledge, but wisdom, passion, integrity, faith, heart affection, and vision.

Each generation must learn to honor those who have gone before, the "pioneers" of the Church who have followed their vision and forged a path for their descendants to walk. Many spiritual parents and grandparents are alive today who ache inside because they have not yet seen the fullness of what God spoke to them 20, 30, or even 50 or more years ago. They long to see their vision fulfilled in their children.

Right before moving from Kansas City, Missouri, to Nashville, Tennessee, Jim was given a striking dream. In it he saw a scrapbook with the year 1988 written on the outside of it. This was a year of much prophetic activity in the Body of Christ and a time of fresh new beginnings.

As Jim opened up the scrapbook in the dream, he read prayers and statements of commitments people had made in 1988. Then, to his surprise, when he turned to the fourth page, he found his own handwriting (and could read it!) where it had the following piercing vow.

"I, Jim Goll, vow to be the unique vessel God created me to be and I vow to do 'all that He created me for.' " Then it continued, *"And I vow to help others be the unique vessels God has created them to be and to help them be all they can be in God!"* Then he could read his own signature as though written in blood!

Yes, God wants us to be secure, unique and multiple! He wants to be fruitful.

MATURE PLANTS AND CORNER PILLARS

As the children honor their parents and grandparents, the synergy of the generations begins to become reality. Thus honor becomes a relational bridge that allows the generational transference to occur. The Lord takes the wisdom of the older generation, combines it with the resources of the middle generation, then mingles it with the zeal of the younger generation. As the younger generation moves out in action, the older ones cheer them on, saying, "Go, go, go! Run with the vision! We will speak counsel, we will speak wisdom, we will speak out of our experience. We will back you with our resources and with our prayers. Run with the vision!"

If this kind of transgenerational harmony and unity is to be fully realized, the modern Church must undergo a paradigm shift of major proportions. The younger generation must learn once again to hold their elders in high honor and respect, no longer dismissing their ideas, values, and counsel as quaint and outmoded relics of the past. For their part, the middle and older generations must be willing to see the younger ones through a different lens; to stop viewing them simply as immature children with little or nothing to offer and recognize both their giftedness and their usefulness in the Kingdom of God. The hearts of the fathers must turn to the children and the hearts of the children to the fathers in recognition of mutual respect and interdependence.

Psalm 144:12 says, "Let our sons in their youth be as grown-up plants, and our daughters as corner pillars fashioned as for a palace." A "grown-up plant" is one that has reached maturity and is ready for full fruitfulness and productivity. Corner pillars are critical structural supports; tear them down and the entire building will collapse.

Usefulness in the Kingdom of God is not gender exclusive. Nor is it an issue of age. It is rather a matter of maturity and calling. Members of the middle and older generations need to recognize that sons and daughters in their youth should be treated with grown-up privileges, not just in the world but in the Church as well. These spiritual children should be equipped, encouraged, and empowered, according to their giftings, to lay hands on the sick, serve as leaders in the church, preach, teach, lead worship, baptize new believers, serve communion, cast out demons, and other areas of ministry and service. Many, because of their ability to think "out of the box," would be very useful in helping to come up with creative strategies for outreach and any number of other issues—strategies that would connect and resonate with members of their own generation who might not be reached any other way.

For too many years the Church has been hampered by a widespread tendency to regard younger believers as "ministers in waiting" who must be held back until they are "old enough" to be useful. Maturity is important, but spiritual maturity for ministry is not always a factor of chronological age. Psalm 144:12 says, "Let our sons *in their youth* be as grown-up plants." It does *not* say, "After they have had ten years of training, and after they have been through four years of Bible college, and after they have been trained in the marketplace for another six and after we finally trust them to not make the same mistakes that we did, we will finally release our sons and daughters to the harvest that has already rotted in the field." There is a vital place for formal education and specialized training, particularly for those called to ministries and marketplace ventures that require it. However, lack of schooling or fear of failure should never of themselves become excuses to deny believers the opportunity to engage in suitable and appropriate ministries, regardless of their age.

WANT A HARVEST?

O ur barns will be filled with every kind of provision. Our sheep will increase by thousands, by tens of thousands in our fields (Psalm 144:13, NIV).

The need of the hour is great. Where are the spiritual fathers and mothers who will pray in the spirit of Elijah, "God, give me a spiritual son or daughter"? Where are the "elders" who will bless those children with their time, knowledge, and every good thing that God has given them? Where are the mentors who will share their life with those children, knowing that generational transfer is about life impartation and not just information? Where will the sons and daughters find spiritual parents who will dream with them and for them, help them tap into their God-given passions and destiny, encourage them and intercede for them?[6]

Responsibility fosters maturity while maturity leads to greater responsibility. The Elijah Revolution calls for a joining of the generations. This means, in part, the promise of the fathers and mothers to treat their sons as grown-up plants and their daughters as corner pillars in the palace of the king. It means the commitment of spiritual parents to speak wisdom and strength and vision into the lives of their "children." It means imparting blessing by a spoken word or a meaningful touch, by giving them a high appraisal of their value, by helping them envision their future in the family of God. It means helping with practical steps, providing necessary resources, and releasing authority to them to accomplish their God-given commission.

Who will rise to the challenge? Who will cry out to the Lord, "I will help take up the fatherless generation! God, give me a spiritual son or daughter!"? *Will you?*

ENDNOTES

1. Tim Ellsworth, "Baptists Adrift in Doctrinal Confusion," *SBC Life* Oct. 2001. 25 Oct. 2001. <http://www.sbclife.org/Articles/2001/10/SLA6.asp>.

2. Jim W. Goll, *The Coming Prophetic Revolution* (Grand Rapids, MI: Chosen Books, 2001), p. 272.

3. Lou Engle, "Restoring the Voice," *Harvest Times*, Vol. 7, No. 2, March/April 2001, p. 11.

4. Abraham had many sons, including Ishmael, by various concubines (see Gen. 16:15; 25:1-6), but only Isaac was born in fulfillment of God's specific promise. It is through Isaac that God's plan was carried forth.

5. Adapted from Lou Engle, "Generational Transfer," *Harvest Times*, Vol. 7, No. 2, March/April 2001, p. 3.

6. Lou Engle, "Generational Transfer," p. 4.

Chapter Four

...For the Nazirites to Arise

Every summer since 1991, during the week prior to Labor Day, a bizarre event has taken place on the Black Rock Desert north of Reno, Nevada. Described by one participant as "a temporary autonomous zone at the edge of eternity,"[1] the Burning Man festival is an annual "celebration" of New Age mysticism and neo-paganism. Attendance has nearly doubled every year until Burning Man now attracts tens of thousands from all 50 states and many foreign countries for a week of "radical self-expression and radical self-reliance."[2] The culmination of the week is the burning of a 40-foot abstract wooden "man" figure, which gives the festival its name.

Rules governing the "radical self-expression" of participants are few, so the Burning Man festival is a wide-open display of hedonistic behavior, including nudity and open sexuality, both "straight" and deviate, and off-the-wall artwork, "theme camps," and drama, much of which exalts satan, mocks God, and demeans Christianity. The festival particularly appeals to New-Agers, occultists, satanists, naturists, and other neo-pagans, as well as people who are simply looking for a place where they can cast off virtually all societal restraints for awhile. All in all, the Burning Man festival is an exercise in rebellion and indulgence.

America is at a critical juncture. The Burning Man festival is but one graphic marker revealing the desperate moral decay and spiritual confusion that has the nation poised on a razor's edge, ready to topple over. There are only two choices: repent or perish.

God would much rather pour out mercy than wrath. To that end He is already raising up His answer to Nevada's "Burning Man" and all it represents—a band of radical warriors who will say "No tolerance!" to evil and stand firmly against compromise, corruption, and idolatry in the land. Committed to a life of total abandonment to Christ and consumed with a passion for holiness, this intrepid company is answering God's call to "stand in the gap" and intercede for the turning of the nation. With their spiritual armor securely in place and their hearts ablaze with holy fire, these servant/soldiers of the King stand ready to be God's own "burning men" (and women) to counter the swelling tide of paganism, pluralism, secularism, immorality, and worldliness that threatens to engulf the country.

The need is great. Just as the Nazarites came forth in ancient Israel to deal with their desperate time, the hour has come in modern America for a new generation of Nazirites to arise. Jim drives this point home in his book, *Wasted on Jesus.*

A fierce conflict is waging in our world today as the forces of evil square off against the forces of good. We are in an age of competing altars: demonic fire versus holy fire, worldly passion versus godly passion. Battle lines have been drawn, and the fight will only intensify as this end-time generation unfolds before us...[But God's] passionate, fiery radicals will make up the first wave assault troops in this cosmic struggle to determine which "controlling substance" will rule our lives. They are the vanguard of a great army consumed with a mighty spiritual passion that is spreading across the worldwide Body of Christ today.[3]

CHILDREN OF DESTINY

In the Scriptures, Nazirites were people of extreme devotion to God who, among other things, left their hair uncut as a mark of their consecration. By their long hair they were saying, in effect, "We are not interested in seeing how little we can get by with in our devotion to God, but how *far* we can go. We are literally exploring the lengths of consecration."

Another characteristic of Nazirites was that they did not drink wine or eat raisins or grapes, all of which represented the sweet pleasures of life. Abstaining in this way from the product of the grape was a Nazirite's way of saying that none of the pleasures of this life could equal the pleasure of knowing God intimately.

Persons of similar bent are arising in the Church today. Although they may not necessarily bear any visible outward mark of their identity, such as long hair, like their counterparts of old, these new radicals for God have a strong sense that they are called and set apart for a holy purpose. God has marked them as Nazirites.

> Nazirites are special people. As the Old Testament reveals, God raises them up when His people are in great distress because they have succumbed to spiritual and moral decay. Time and time again throughout Israel's history, Nazirites turned the tide of spiritual and national degeneration.[4]

Could the same be true today? God wants to spare America, not judge her. Can anything be done to turn the tide of the nation's "spiritual and moral decay," to reverse America's "spiritual and national degeneration," symbolized so graphically by Nevada's Burning Man?

For a long time Lou Engle has preached about the "burning man" and the need for God to raise up His own "burning men" to help turn the nation. Several months before *The Call DC* he heard about a powerful prophetic encounter related to the whole issue.

> A young man called a friend of mine and related to him a dream he had experienced. This young man had no connection with me at all and had never heard any of my "burning man" stuff. He saw a large open field filled with young people coming to pray. Suddenly, a 4-story tall figure of a burning man appeared on the field, and instantly all the kids ran and scattered for protection. In his dream the young man ran behind the pavilion and began calling out to God, "What do we do, Lord? How do we break the power of this burning man?" Then he saw a lunch box with the words "Nazirite Serendipity" on the side. He took the lunch box and threw it at the burning man, which disintegrated.

> After I heard about this dream, I pondered over it for a long time, not sure of what it meant. Serendipity refers to a fortuitous moment or situations or people unexpectedly coming together to an agreeable or valuable outcome. It's kind of like a divine appointment.

> A few days before *The Call DC*, the Holy Spirit gave me the interpretation. He said to me, "Lou, these young Nazirites are coming to the Mall. I want you to call them to give their lunches away for 40 days—to throw them at the burning man—and to pray for their schools. Issue the challenge for tens of thousands

of kids to use their lunch time for 40 days to pray for a great awakening in America."

So that's what we did. We called on those young people to throw away their lunches and fast and pray for America, and many of them rose to the challenge.

Across the country thousands of Christian young people are beginning to discover their destiny in the Lord. Many have been captivated by the vision and passion to rise up and help shape the spiritual and moral future of their nation. In ancient Israel Nazirites often were the hinge of history, a crucial part of God's strategy to bring revival and restoration to His people. Today, as then, God is looking for Nazirite kids who are willing to be the hinge upon whom He can turn a nation back to Him.

RADICAL FOR GOD

Whether found in ancient Israel or in the twenty-first century Church, Nazirites share a burning zeal for God and a consuming jealousy for the glory and reputation of His holy name. Nothing fires their spirit more than to live in radical abandonment to Him. They find their supreme joy in walking in intimate fellowship with God and in obeying His will in all things.

Nazirite tradition goes back a long way. This religious order of men and women arose very early in Israel's history, at least as early as the time of the Mosaic Law.[5] The biblical guidelines for Nazirites are found in the sixth chapter of Numbers:

Again the Lord spoke to Moses, saying, "Speak to the sons of Israel, and say to them, 'When a man or woman makes a special vow, the vow of a Nazirite, to dedicate himself to the Lord, he shall abstain from wine and strong drink; he shall drink no vinegar, whether made from wine or strong drink, neither shall he drink any grape juice, nor eat fresh or dried grapes. All the days of his separation he shall not eat anything that is produced by the grape vine, from the seeds even to the skin. All the days of his vow of separation no razor shall pass over his head. He shall be holy until the days are fulfilled for which he separated himself to the Lord; he shall let the locks of hair on his head grow long. All the days of his separation to the Lord he shall not go near to a dead person. He shall not make himself unclean for his father or for his mother, for his brother or for his sister, when they die, because his separation to God is on his head. All the days of his separation he is holy to the Lord.'...This is the law of the Nazirite who vows his offering to the Lord according to his separation, in addition to what else he can afford; according to his vow which he takes, so he shall do according to the law of his separation" (Numbers 6:1-8,21).

From the beginning, Nazirites had a powerful influence on the spirit and conscience of the nation.

God raised up these young men and women to draw attention to the spiritual unholiness of His people and to protest the fact that false gods had captured their hearts. The Nazirites were the Generation X-treme of their day—the Generation Y-zer! They became the role models for their generation.[6]

Although in most instances the Nazirite vow was a temporary commitment for a specific time and purpose, the Bible does tell of people who were lifelong Nazirites. Samson was set apart as a Nazirite even before he was born. Throughout his life he delivered Israel from the hands of the Philistines. Samuel was a lifelong Nazirite. Consecrated to the Lord before birth like Samson, Samuel was in a rather unique position. In addition to being a priest, he also was the last of Israel's judges and the first of a long line of prophets. Samuel anointed the first two kings of Israel—Saul and David—and by his own example kept the hearts of the people focused on the Lord. John the Baptist was a lifelong Nazirite who appeared as a "voice shouting in the wilderness"—the first prophet Israel had seen in 400 years—to announce the coming of the Messiah. Through his lifestyle and his message John awakened and conditioned a spiritually dulled nation to turn back to God and to await with great anticipation the soon arrival of their King.

Samson, Samuel, and John the Baptist shared a radical devotion to God that affected the destiny of the entire nation. Although Samson's personal weaknesses and self-indulgence brought about his downfall, in the end he renewed his Nazirite consecration to God. At the moment of his death Samson killed more Philistines than he had throughout his entire life.

Nazirite consecration was an opportunity for non-priests to make a radical commitment to God. Although the Jewish priesthood was limited by law to men from the tribe of Levi, the Nazirite vow was open to anyone, male or female, of any tribe. Nazirite consecration was for the "normal joes" who wanted to do something special for God, to go to an extreme for Him; ordinary people who wanted an extraordinary separation to God in a life of radical holiness. A closer look at the Nazirite vow in Numbers chapter 6 will help reveal what fired the hearts of these radicals for God.

MARKED BY GOD

The Nazirite vow consisted essentially of three restrictions to be observed by those making the commitment: abstention from all products of the grape, leaving one's hair uncut, and avoiding all contact with anything that was dead. At first glance these conditions may seem highly legalistic. In reality, however, Nazirites took them up willingly as outward marks of their inward consecration, external symbols of their extreme love for God.

First, a Nazirite would not eat grapes or raisins or drink wine or grape juice. Why not? What does abstaining from these things have to do with radical separation to God? The answer lies in what they represent. In *The Call Revolution* Lou Engle wrote:

> Wine is the symbol of natural joy—grapes, the source of God-given sweetness and pleasure. For the Hebrew, the enjoyment of grapes was a legitimate pleasure. The Nazirite, however, could not, would not, even touch these things. Why? Here's the heart of the Nazirite vow: *These holy lovers of God denied themselves the legitimate pleasure of this life in exchange for the extreme pleasure of knowing God.*[7]

By abstaining from grapes and all their products Nazirites were saying to God, "All our fountains of joy are in You." They willingly renounced the good things of the earth for the greater joy of focusing exclusively on the glorious things of God. This was extreme self-denial as an expression of extreme love. As such it symbolized a Nazirite's commitment to the highest degree of purity, "a purity that freely chooses to abstain from what is acceptable, for the purpose of gaining what is otherwise unobtainable."[8] Nazirites would not allow anything to occupy their thoughts or hold their affection more than God. He was their everything.

Renouncing wine and grape products had another purpose as well. By avoiding anything that was fermented, a Nazirite was saying, "I'm going to stay away from anything, any other spirit, that might possess me or control my faculties, so that I can be possessed by God." This is the same attitude that Paul had in mind when he wrote, "And do not get drunk with wine, for that is dissipation, but be filled with the Spirit" (Eph. 5:18).

The second and most visible mark of a Nazirite was uncut hair. This made them stand out plainly in the midst of the people. Long hair symbolized the strength of their commitment to God, made them accountable to others for their faithfulness to their vow, and served as a public mark of their consecration.[9] Keeping their hair long reminded Nazirites that the eyes of both God and men were on them. It encouraged them to walk carefully before the Lord.

Nazirites were forbidden by their vow to come into contact with anything that was dead, including members of their own family. This prohibition symbolized two things. First, it spoke of abstaining from anything that would bring death to their soul, anything that could usurp their passion or pollute their power. Secondly, it referred to renouncing dead works and legalism. This kind of sacrifice, this kind of extreme commitment to God, was not to be performed as a dead religious duty, but out of passion. To a Nazirite, religion was not cold formalism and dead tradition but a relationship with a living God that was full of vibrant life and characterized by eager obedience. Nazirites sacrificed themselves and served the Lord not because they had to but because they wanted to.

NAZIRITES, ARISE!

Historically, Nazirites always seemed to show up just when there was great religious upheaval in the land. With their long hair and extreme ways Nazirites were the "holy hippies" of their day, a countercultural movement of holy warriors committed to waging a godly counterattack against the spiritual rebellion that characterized most of the rest of their nation. God raised them up as preservatives for a society that was sinking rapidly into spiritual pollution and immorality. These young revolutionaries would stand in the gap as the "salt" of the covenant for the preservation of the nation. As counterculturalists they went against the popular tide and trends, saying, "No! We refuse to bow down to your gods. We refuse to compromise. We will not quit until every altar to Baal is gone from the land."

Because Nazirites were generally respected for their passion and depth of commitment, many of them were also effective leaders of the people: "Then Deborah and Barak the son of Abinoam sang on that day, saying, 'That the leaders led in Israel, that the people volunteered, bless the Lord!' " (Judg. 5:1-2) The Hebrew word translated "led" is related to a root that literally means to "loosen the locks." In other words, when the leaders of Israel "let their hair down," the people volunteered and followed them into battle. These were Nazirites who had made a vow for holy war against Sisera and his army. Like William "Braveheart" Wallace of Scotland, they loosened their locks and ran to the battle. When the Nazirites lead, the rest of the people volunteer willingly.

Nazirites are arising in America, young kids who are burning with a zeal for God and a jealousy for His good name, who are ready to stand in the gap for their country and say, "Enough of the prophets of Baal! Enough of all the trash coming out of Hollywood and the television studios! No more tolerance and no more compromise! Enough of abortion, drugs, and violent crime that are destroying our generation! Enough of laws that remove God and the prophetic voice of the Church from the public arena! We will not run, we will not give in, we will not quit until all the 'altars to Baal' are removed from our land!"

That's the kind of zeal that is needed to tear down the wicked forces of this nation and rebuild her godly foundations.

America needs a Nazirite generation as a counterculture to the prevailing trends of society.

The time has come for Nazirites to arise in America to fast and pray for revival and to stand firm against the forces of darkness and godlessness in the land. A Nazirite vow is a very serious commitment. No one should make such a vow who has not thoroughly prayed it through, has become convinced that it is God's will, and has counted the cost of that vow.

Like the Nazirites in the fifth chapter of Judges who led the people into battle, America needs a Nazirite army, an army of the dawn that in the darkest hour of the nation's history will gather to fast and pray for the coming of a new day. This is the dawning of a new Jesus revolution.

In the past, Nazirites often were the hinge of history in Israel. America today is at the hinge of history; the door could swing either way. God is calling forth a massive transgenerational movement of youth and adults who will fast and pray, take Nazirite vows, and break through into the heavens.

Psalm 11:3 says, "If the foundations are destroyed, what can the righteous do?" They can call on God and offer themselves as living sacrifices, as altars upon whom God's fire can fall. If the righteous will fast and pray, God Himself will shake the prophets of Baal, send fire from Heaven, and turn the nation. Casual measures are not enough. The need of the hour demands something more: radical abandonment to God and extreme commitment to His holiness. This is the Nazirite call. This is the spirit of Elijah, and it is sorely needed in this hour.

Some time back Lou received from one of these young firebrands a poem that captures perfectly the consuming fire that blazes in the hearts of God's new Nazirites. Let his words be the battle cry for the army of the Lord. Nazirites, arise!

FOR SUCH A TIME

I was fashioned for this day
I was born just for this hour
A day of revolution
An invasion of Your power

We're John the Baptist signals
Posted high up on a hill
Lifting trumpet voices
And doing all Your will

My heart was made for burning
My destiny extreme
Called to be a Nazirite
A faith and fire machine

I'm fasting in the desert
And making straight the path
Proclaiming by Your Spirit
"Mercy triumphs over wrath!"

I'm laying down my future
In worship at Your feet
I'm calling for revival
To fill our nation's streets

I'm lifting up my voice
To God who answers prayer
"Make me the hinge of hist'ry!"
And He answers
"Become it if you dare!"

To see the Lamb exalted
And His reward secured
I'll live a life of sacrifice
And let His voice be heard

For such a time as this
And for this very hour

God's called a generation
To be channels of His power

John the Baptist company
With Elijah in their blood
Burning in the desert
So that God will send a flood[10]

ENDNOTES

1. George Otis, Jr., "Invasion From the Dark Side," *Charisma*, Mar. 1997, 4 Jan. 2002. <http://www.charismamag.com/march97/cm197105.htm>.

2. Description from the official website of the Burning Man festival: <http://www.burningman.com>.

3. Jim Goll, *Wasted on Jesus* (Shippensburg, PA: Destiny Image Publishers, Inc., 2000) pp. 1-2.

4. Lou Engle, *Digging the Wells of Revival* (Shippensburg, PA: Revival Press, an imprint of Destiny Image Publishers, Inc., 1998), p. 196.

5. Dr. Ché H. Ahn and Lou Engle, *The Call Revolution* (Colorado Springs, CO: Wagner Publications, 2001), p. 24.

6. Ahn and Engle, *The Call Revolution*, pp. 24-25.

7. Ahn and Engle, *The Call Revolution*, pp. 26-27.

8. Engle, *Digging the Wells of Revival*, p. 197.

9. Ahn and Engle, *The Call Revolution*, p. 28.

10. Sylvia M. Barnhart.

Part Two

The Battle
of All Times

Chapter Five

The Spirit of Elijah vs. Jezebel

Throughout the land battle lines are being drawn for the next skirmish of the greatest war in history. The conflict is not new; it is in fact as old as time. On one side stands the adversary, a demonic spirit that seeks to destroy the family, morality, integrity, and every element of a godly society. Its goal is to neutralize legitimate leadership and veil human eyes to the reality of the one true God, and its weapons are guile, deceit, manipulation, and control. Although this spirit of darkness is genderless, manifesting in the lives of men and women alike and appearing throughout the ages in many forms of adaptive deception, this fiendish seducer is commonly identified as the "Jezebel" spirit.

Arrayed against this demonic force is the army of the King of kings, the Church, anointed by the grace of God and endowed by the Holy Spirit with His power and authority. The Church, bearing as she does the same prophetic presence that was on Elijah of old, stands in absolute antithesis to the Jezebel spirit. Elijah and Jezebel were mortal enemies.

Today the Jezebel spirit exercises a major role in the power of evil over the nations of the world. Many of the ideologies in America, the "mind-molders" that shape the opinions, values, and worldview of young and old alike, are in thrall to this satanic influence. Hollywood is permeated with it. So is the music, entertainment, and information industries. Most of America's public schools and secular colleges and universities are bastions of a thoroughly humanistic worldview that is anti-God and anti-Christian.

Under the Jezebel spirit's destructive and manipulative sway, the government in recent years has enacted laws and policies that tear away at the social, moral, and spiritual fiber of the country. A generation ago, prayer was legislated out of public schools. Legalized abortion on demand has demeaned the value of human life. The Ten Commandments became the ten suggestions. Laws restricting free public expression by people of faith, particularly Christians, have made a mockery of the state's so-called "neutrality" in matters of religion. Biblical values and principles are under attack at every turn.

This is not to condemn the media, the schools, the government, or any other industry or institution in and of themselves. It is a reminder that the "struggle is not against flesh and blood, but against the rulers, against the powers, against the world forces of this darkness, against the spiritual forces of wickedness in the heavenly places" (Eph. 6:12). Institutions and industries are not the enemy. Neither are the people who work in them. The enemy is that foul, deceptive, and devilish spirit that has gotten a stranglehold on many of them and is intent on capturing entire generations under demonic bondage.

In this cosmic, age-old struggle, the Church is by no means immune. Through cunning and subtle deception the Jezebel spirit can gain a foothold among an unwary body of believers where it proceeds to corrupt faith, distort true worship, and undermine God-ordained authority. Following the stratagem of "divide and conquer," the Jezebel spirit aims to dilute and trivialize the exercise of authentic spiritual gifts and to effectively silence the Church's prophetic voice.

The only answer for this Jezebel influence in the Church or anywhere else is true discernment, complete "rug-eating" repentance, and victory through the blood of Jesus Christ. Spiritually sensitive and burdened believers everywhere should go before the Lord in identificational repentance on behalf of the entire Body of Christ for its part in allowing the Jezebel influence to become so pervasive in the land. Coupled with this should be intense intercession for the breaking of these demonic strongholds, so that the words of Isaiah 60:18 will come to pass: "Violence will not be heard again in your land, nor devastation or destruction within your borders; but you will call your walls salvation, and your gates praise."

Unprecedented prayer and fasting on the part of God's people are in order if the Jezebel spirit in America is to be broken. Through a piercing dream in December 2000, Lou received a word from the Lord that said, "No one is targeting false ideologies with massive fasting and prayer." This has now become the central compass point guiding the plans for all future mass prayer rallies under the umbrella of *The Call*. Jesus said that there are some demonic forces that cannot be cast out except by prayer and fasting (see Mt. 17:21).

America and the nations face either judgment or revival. How the Church responds in this hour will be critical in determining which way the scale tips. The Elijah Revolution is focused on exposing and breaking the Jezebel influence and bringing restoration and revival to the land. It happened in Elijah's day, and it can happen today!

AHAB AND JEZEBEL

One of the primary ways the Jezebel spirit gains inroads to power is by deceiving and corrupting legitimate leadership. Corrupt leaders cause their people to go astray as well. "If a ruler pays attention to falsehood, all his ministers become wicked" (Prov. 29:12). "Ministers" could also be translated as "servants." The Hebrew word refers primarily to a high order of service[1] but can also mean service of a menial nature.[2] Evil in leaders affects not only their officials but the common people as well. One of the best biblical examples of this is seen in the reign of Ahab, king of Israel, and his wife, Jezebel.

> *Now Ahab the son of Omri became king over Israel in the thirty-eighth year of Asa king of Judah, and Ahab the son of Omri reigned over Israel in Samaria twenty-two years. And Ahab the son of Omri did evil in the sight of the Lord more than all who were before him. And it came about, as though it had been a trivial thing for him to walk in the sins of Jeroboam the son of Nebat, that he married Jezebel the daughter of Ethbaal king of the Sidonians, and went to serve Baal and worshiped him. So he erected an altar for Baal in the house of Baal, which he built in Samaria. And Ahab also made the Asherah. Thus Ahab did more to provoke the Lord God of Israel than all the kings of Israel who were before him* (1 Kings 16:29-33).

Israel was established as a nation holy to the Lord. He was their God and they were His people. Yet the Israelites turned away from God and descended into gross immorality and idolatry, due in large part to the destructive example of corrupt and compromising rulers.

Ahab was one of the worst. Contrary to God's command against the Israelites intermarrying with the people of the surrounding nations, Ahab took the pagan princess Jezebel as his wife. Jezebel came from a religious family; her father, Ethbaal, was named for their god. They and their people were Sidonians, a nation of hunters who worshiped Baal and Ashteroth, the goddess of love, fertility, and war. Their religion was essentially a fertility cult that involved child sacrifice, lewd and licentious worship, and fertility rites that were both heterosexual and homosexual in nature.

Jezebel was very religious and converted Ahab. Her religion, however, was a false religion, an idolatrous religion that worshiped the work of human hands, a religion of form without power. Ahab was a man of weak character who took sin lightly and showed utter disregard for the laws of God. Under Jezebel's wily influence, he was drawn deeply and thoroughly into idolatry.

That's how the Jezebel spirit works. Jezebel can have little influence without an Ahab. The name *Jezebel* means "no cohabitation." Jezebel could not cohabit; she had to take over. That was her nature. Even in marriage, Jezebel could not cohabit; she had to be in control. Her weapons were many—seduction, coercion, manipulation, humiliation, deception, flattery, slander—whatever it took to gain that control. Ahab was no match for her. Together they led the people of Israel deeper into the mire of immorality and idolatry from which they never completely recovered.

In the midst of a land established with godly roots, Jezebel killed every prophet of the Lord she could get her hands on. Apart from Elijah, none survived except for 100 whom Obadiah, an official in Ahab's court, hid in two caves and took care of (see 1 Kings 18:3-4). Jezebel also supported an entire school of 450 prophets of Baal and 400 prophets of the Asherah, who ate at her table (see 1 Kings 18:19). The spiritual corruption under Jezebel and Ahab was so thorough that eventually, out of a population in Israel of perhaps 10 million, only 7,000 had never bowed down to Baal (see 1 Kings 19:18).

Whenever the Jezebel spirit rises up in a nation, it seeks to destroy the prophetic anointing on the land, rob the people of their godly inheritance, turn them aside from their godly roots, and pull them down into spiritual blindness and bondage to the powers of darkness.

ELIJAH AND JEZEBEL

The ungodly influence of Jezebel and Ahab did not go unchallenged. No matter when or where the Jezebel spirit struts onto the stage, God always has a champion waiting in the wings, ready to enter and do battle. God always raises up an "Elijah" to go "head to head" with Jezebel.

In First Kings 17:1, Elijah comes before Ahab and announces a drought throughout the land that will continue until he says otherwise. Already the boldness of God's anointed messenger is clear. The gauntlet has been thrown down; the contest has been joined. Suddenly, two mighty forces have arisen to contend with each other, and to the victor goes the nation. Elijah has come forward in the power and authority of God and with a prophetic anointing to stand in the gap and oppose Jezebel and everything she stands for. Ahab may be the king, but Jezebel runs the show. Ahab is little more than a puppet, and Jezebel pulls the strings. That's always the way it is with a Jezebel spirit; Jezebel must control.

One of Jezebel's first campaigns was to wipe out the prophets of God because they proclaimed the Word of the Lord and called for repentance. The spirit of Jezebel hates the Word of God because it has the power to transform people and nations. Jezebel's assault on the prophets of God was so relentless that the few who remained survived only by hiding out in caves.

Then Elijah appeared on Mount Carmel and challenged the prophets of Baal to a contest (see 1 Kings 18:17-40). After Baal's prophets utterly failed to get their god's attention, Elijah called on the Lord God, who sent fire from Heaven to consume the sacrifice that Elijah had prepared. In the wake of this demonstration that exposes Baal as a false god, the Israelites reaffirm their faith in the Lord as God, and Elijah slays all the prophets of Baal.

Jezebel killed God's prophets, but Elijah killed Jezebel's prophets—those who ate at her table and received her support. Two contenders were at war here, and they were both after each other's prophets. Both were filled with fiery zeal. Jezebel worked and schemed to silence the authentic prophetic voice of God's people and to destroy the nation's godly roots. Elijah, by his own testimony, was "very zealous for the Lord, the God of hosts" (1 Kings 19:10a). He was possessed by a prophetic zeal that would not tolerate the presence of Jezebel in his land, in his life, or in the lives of his people.

Such zeal for God alone is the only kind of spirit that can turn America back to Him. The people of God must be fired with the spirit of Elijah. They must burn with a holy passion for the things of God: His name, His reputation, His purposes, His presence, the welfare of His people, and for His glory to fill the earth. The hearts of the fathers must be turned to the children and the hearts of the children to the fathers. Godly fatherhood and motherhood must be restored to the Church for the raising up of spiritual sons and daughters.

Jezebel did not take kindly to Elijah's execution of the prophets of Baal. As soon as she got word of the incident on Mount Carmel, she put Elijah on notice: "So may the gods do to me and even more, if I do not make your life as the life of one of them by tomorrow about this time" (1 Kings 19:2b).

For some reason, at this point Elijah's courage and boldness failed him for a time. Fear and intimidation of Jezebel suddenly gripped his heart. Elijah didn't hang around to give Jezebel the opportunity to carry out her threat. He ran for his life. Forty days later, during which he fasted and prayed, Elijah found himself on Mount Horeb. Elijah's fear had distorted his perspective of reality, causing him to think he was all alone in his struggle. On the mountain the Lord spoke to Elijah not in wind, earthquake, or fire, but the "sound of a gentle blowing" (see 1 Kings 19:11-12).

And it came about when Elijah heard it, that he wrapped his face in his mantle, and went out and stood in the entrance of the cave. And behold, a voice came to him and said, "What are you doing here, Elijah?" Then he said, "I have been very zealous for the Lord, the God of hosts; for the sons of Israel have forsaken Thy covenant, torn down Thine altars and killed Thy prophets with the sword. And I alone am left; and they seek my life, to take it away." And the Lord said to him, "Go, return on your way to the wilderness of Damascus, and when you have arrived, you shall anoint Hazael king over Syria; and Jehu the son of Nimshi you shall anoint king over Israel; and Elisha the son of Shaphat of Abel-meholah you shall anoint as prophet in your place. And it shall come about, the one who escapes from the sword of Hazael, Jehu shall put to death, and the one who escapes from the sword of Jehu, Elisha shall put to death. Yet I will leave 7000 in Israel, all the knees that have not bowed to Baal and every mouth that has not kissed him" (1 Kings 19:13-18).

God's soft voice gently set His prophet straight and redirected his ministry. Elijah's 40-day fast in the wilderness refreshed his spirit, prepared him for his encounter with God, and broke the fear of Jezebel off of his life. From this point on he never ran from Jezebel again.

NABOTH AND JEZEBEL

Jezebel's treachery toward an innocent and righteous man named Naboth marked the beginning of the end for her and Ahab. This incident from the twenty-first chapter of First Kings provides an excellent capsule view of the Jezebel spirit at work.

Naboth owned a vineyard next to Ahab's palace in Jezreel. It was part of his family's inheritance. Ahab desired the vineyard for a vegetable garden. He offered to buy it from Naboth or to trade it for a better vineyard somewhere else, but Naboth was unwilling to part with it.

Ahab returned to his palace "sullen and vexed" because Naboth had refused to sell his vineyard (1 Kings 21:4). He went to bed and refused all food. The king of Israel was pouting because he didn't get his way! That's how he was when Jezebel found him. After Ahab told her what had happened, she comforted him by saying, "Do you now reign over Israel? Arise, eat bread, and let your heart be joyful; I will give you the vineyard of Naboth the Jezreelite" (1 Kings 21:7b).

When Ahab couldn't get what he wanted, he started whining and wallowing in depression and self-pity. That's one of the effects of the Jezebel influence. Self-pity leads to unhealthy introspection and preoccupation, which lead to anger, greed, bitterness, and other sins of body and mind. This kind of thinking quickly becomes a pattern that opens the door wide for more of the same. Ahab played right into Jezebel's controlling clutches. "Don't worry, sweetie," she said. "Just leave it to me, and I'll get Naboth's vineyard for you." The Jezebel spirit controls by charm, allure, scorn, sarcasm, treachery—whatever is needed at the moment.

Jezebel lost no time in putting her scheme into action.

So she wrote letters in Ahab's name and sealed them with his seal, and sent letters to the elders and to the nobles who were living with Naboth in his city. Now she wrote in the letters, saying, "Proclaim a fast, and seat Naboth at the head of the people; and seat two worthless men before him, and let them testify against him, saying, 'You cursed God and the king.' Then take him out and stone him to death" (1 Kings 21:8-10).

Jezebel usurped her husband's authority by writing her own decree and signing it with the king's name. She manipulated control of leadership as a power base to cloak her evil designs under the guise of legitimate authority. Jezebel even had no qualms about falsely invoking God's name and wrapping her fiendish plot in the garments of religious piety. The queen's instructions were carried out quickly, and soon Naboth was dead.

When Ahab heard the news, he got up and hurried to Naboth's vineyard to take possession of it. There he was met by Elijah, who had a word from the Lord for the king:

> *"...Thus says the Lord, 'Have you murdered, and also taken possession?....In the place where the dogs licked up the blood of Naboth the dogs shall lick up your blood, even yours.'...Behold, I will bring evil upon you, and will utterly sweep you away, and will cut off from Ahab every male, both bond and free in Israel...because of the provocation with which you have provoked Me to anger, and because you have made Israel sin. And of Jezebel also has the Lord spoken, saying, 'The dogs shall eat Jezebel in the district of Jezreel.' The one belonging to Ahab, who dies in the city, the dogs shall eat, and the one who dies in the field the birds of heaven shall eat"* (1 Kings 21:19, 21-24).

Although Ahab did not personally participate in the plot against Naboth, he went along with Jezebel's plan and therefore shared in her guilt. God pronounced sure and certain judgment on them not only because their sins had provoked Him to anger but also because *they had made Israel sin.* Anyone who leads others into sin and away from the one true God incurs His wrath and judgment, which are inevitable unless that person repents.

It is to Ahab's credit that his response to Elijah's prophecy of judgment was to humble himself before the Lord by fasting and wearing sackcloth, which was a symbol of mourning and submission. As a result, God withheld His full judgment on Ahab's family until after the king's death so he would not witness it with his own eyes (see 1 Kings 21:27-29). In this God demonstrated His grace and mercy, available to anyone who comes to Him in humbleness of heart. Ahab, though, died in battle three years later.

Although the breaking of the Jezebelic influence in Israel began with Elijah, it was not completed until the next generation. Rarely is a Jezebel spirit broken quickly or easily; it requires time and sacrificial living, including prayer and fasting. That is why generational transfer and the joining of the generations are so important. It was that way then, and it will be that way today.

JEHU AND JEZEBEL

As God had instructed him, Elijah anointed Elisha as his prophetic successor. Although Jezebel had killed most of the Lord's prophets, by the end of Elijah's ministry a new generation of prophets had arisen (much like today), inspired by his example and fired with his spirit. God also had told Elijah to anoint Jehu as king of Israel, but it was actually Elisha who carried this out. There is a proper time for everything, even for the fulfillment of God's instructions.

Fourteen years after Ahab's death, the time was right. Joram, the second of Ahab's sons to sit as king of Israel since his death, was at war with the Arameans. Elisha dispatched one of his protégés, one of the "sons of the prophets" on a mission to anoint Jehu as king. As soon as the young man had completed his task, he was to flee (see 2 Kings 9:1-3).

Jehu was a captain of the army who had a passion for God and a smoldering fire in his heart to rid his country of sin and idolatry. When Elisha's messenger found Jehu, he poured oil on his head and said,

> *Thus says the Lord, the God of Israel, "I have anointed you king over the people of the Lord, even over Israel. And you shall strike the house of Ahab your master, that I may avenge the blood of My servants the prophets, and the blood of all the servants of the Lord, at the hand of Jezebel. For the whole house of Ahab shall perish, and I will cut off from Ahab every male person both bond and free in*

*Israel....And the dogs shall eat Jezebel in the territory of
Jezreel, and none shall bury her"* (2 Kings 9:6b-8,10a).

Jehu wasted no time; his appointed hour had come. The
first thing he did was to assassinate Joram, king of Israel.
Joram rode in a chariot to meet Jehu, who was waiting in
Naboth's old vineyard.

> *...when Joram saw Jehu, that he said, "Is it peace, Jehu?"
> And he answered, "What peace, so long as the harlotries
> of your mother Jezebel and her witchcrafts are so many?"
> So Joram reined about and fled and said to Ahaziah,
> "There is treachery, O Ahaziah!" And Jehu drew his bow
> with his full strength and shot Joram between his arms;
> and the arrow went through his heart, and he sank in his
> chariot* (2 Kings 9:22-24).

The fact that this encounter took place in Naboth's field
was no accident. It was deliberate on Jehu's part.

> *Then Jehu said to Bidkar his officer, "Take him up and
> cast him into the property of the field of Naboth the Jezreel-
> ite, for I remember when you and I were riding together
> after Ahab his father, that the Lord laid this oracle
> against him: 'Surely I have seen yesterday the blood of
> Naboth and the blood of his sons,' says the Lord, 'and I
> will repay you in this property,' says the Lord. Now then,
> take and cast him into the property, according to the word
> of the Lord"* (2 Kings 9:25-26).

Next, Jehu proceeded to kill Ahaziah, the evil king of
Judah who was in league with Joram, then made his way to
Jezreel to confront Jezebel. Payday had arrived.

> *When Jehu came to Jezreel, Jezebel heard of it, and she
> painted her eyes and adorned her head, and looked out the
> window. And as Jehu entered the gate, she said, "Is it well,
> Zimri, your master's murderer?" Then he lifted up his face
> to the window and said, "Who is on my side? Who?" And
> two or three officials looked down at him. And he said,*

"Throw her down." So they threw her down, and some of her blood was sprinkled on the wall and on the horses, and he trampled her under foot. When he came in, he ate and drank; and he said, "See now to this cursed woman and bury her, for she is a king's daughter." And they went to bury her, but they found no more of her than the skull and the feet and the palms of her hands. Therefore they returned and told him. And he said, "This is the word of the Lord, which He spoke by His servant Elijah the Tishbite, saying, 'In the property of Jezreel the dogs shall eat the flesh of Jezebel; and the corpse of Jezebel shall be as dung on the face of the field in the property of Jezreel, so they cannot say, "This is Jezebel" ' " (2 Kings 9:30-37).

Jezebel was entrenched in power in Israel for many years. Her evil influence permeated the land, seemingly invincible. Yet, at God's appointed time and by the hand of His appointed instrument, her destruction was total and absolute.

No Toleration!

One of the greatest challenges facing the Body of Christ today is how to deal with the powerful influence of the Jezebel spirit that is so pervasive throughout the land. Part of the difficulty stems from the fact that this same spirit has gained a foothold within the Church. Acquiescence, toleration, and inattention on the part of many have allowed the enemy to sneak into the camp and cause strife, division, and confusion. "Jezebel" attacks relationships, finances, health, and reputation. Because it seeks to kill or cut off the influence of the true prophetic voice, the Jezebel spirit lies behind much of the current epidemic of pastors and other spiritual leaders being fired or falling into sexual sin. Under the sway of "Jezebel," a church loses its vision and vitality, becoming sidetracked from its mission of proclaiming the gospel of Jesus Christ and focusing instead on secondary issues.

At the same time that it is muzzling the voice of the Church and hobbling its effectiveness in ministry, the Jezebel spirit is working to gain preeminence in the segments of society that are the most influential "mind-shapers" of the young: the entertainment industry, the media, the educational system, and the family. It is the driving force in America behind both the enormous divorce rate and the thriving abortion industry. "Jezebel" is after the children, to snuff out an entire generation and prevent the transfer of godly heritage, values, and principles.

The nations are in deep trouble, but there is hope. Elijah appeared in his day to confront, expose, and destroy Jezebel. His influence gave rise to Elisha, a spiritual son with a "double portion" anointing, and to Jehu, a holy warrior whose passion for God burned like a cleansing fire. In the same way, God raises up "Elijahs," "Elishas," and "Jehus" in every generation to do battle with Jezebel.

The spirit of Elijah is alive in the land, rising up in the hearts of more and more believers, a spirit that declares "No toleration!" for Jezebel's influence. "No toleration for the 'prophets of Baal'—the New Age gurus, the priests of pluralism and neo-paganism, and the sages of secularism and humanism! No toleration for the purveyors of filth, immorality, and godlessness who flood the homes and minds of much of the world through television, music, and movies!" God wants to save them, but He also wants to destroy the demonic spirit that controls them and infects millions of people, particularly young people. The Holy Spirit wants to cleanse these "mind molders" and then turn right around and invade them with a new breed of godly influences.

But this is a war to the end—Elijah versus Jezebel—and to the victor goes the soul of the nations. Unless the hearts of the fathers are restored to the children and the hearts of the children to the fathers, Jezebel will continue to win. However, a divine revolution is at hand, a turnaround that can transform the country and reshape the destiny of the people.

There is a new spirit of prayer and fasting blowing through the Church that can make the critical difference. Elijah was a man of prayer and fasting. He prayed and fire from Heaven fell, igniting a revival in Israel. He fasted for 40 days and the spirit and power of Jezebel over his life were broken, setting in motion the events and circumstances that led to her complete destruction. It can happen today as it happened then.

How About Today?

What would happen if tens of thousands or hundreds of thousands of spiritual fathers and mothers in America and beyond committed themselves to prayer and fasting for the breaking of the spirit of Jezebel over their lives and the lives of their children? What would happen if they turned off their televisions and other entertainment and for 40 days sought the face of God for a spiritual and moral reversal in America? What would happen if they interceded for their children for 40 days, that a "double portion" spirit would be poured out on their "Elishas" and "Jehus"? What would happen? Nothing short of a revolution.

The Elijah Revolution links three generations in prayer and fasting because one generation is not sufficient to win out over the Jezebel spirit. Half-measures will not do. It is not enough simply to have the fire of revival. That fire must be transferred to the next generation, because it is only the sons and daughters who will rise into the double portion anointing.

If America is to move forward into godlikeness, the ancient boundaries of moral purity and spiritual integrity must be rebuilt. The endtimes Church, the Church of the "Elijah" generation, must take the lead. It is time for the Body of Christ to return to committed radical righteous living in a day of moral decadence. It's time for passion and sacrifice to call forth radical change.

God is zealous to destroy the works of Jezebel in the land, and He will begin by purifying His own house. He is searching the hearts and minds of believers for any attitude or mind-set that tolerates the spirit of Jezebel, anything that opens the door to manipulation, control, and rebellion. God is saying to His children, "I want to break that spirit off of your life. I will not tolerate Jezebel any longer."

The question is not will God bless America, but will America bless God! He wants to break the influence of Jezebel in the land. But He is waiting for those of kindred spirit with Him to arise, those of the "Elijah" generation, who boldly cry out, "O Lord...today let it be known that Thou art God...that this people may know that Thou...art God, and that Thou hast turned their heart back again" (1 Kings 18:36b-37).

What is at stake ultimately is the Church's God-given authority over the nations to spread the gospel of Jesus Christ with power into all the world. The Jezebel spirit fights tooth and nail against this. Those devilish teeth must be pulled out and those clawing nails must be broken.

Lord, let the fire fall! Break the spirit of Jezebel from the land and draw this great nation back to You! Let the sons and daughters of the double portion anointing arise to stand in the gap committed to holy lives of no compromise and no toleration of evil or corruption. Cause their hearts to be filled with nothing but burning passion for You and You alone! Let this be the hour; turn the nations once more to You! Let the Call be heard! Let the Call be answered!

ENDNOTES

1. R. Laird Harris, Gleason L. Archer, Jr., and Bruce K. Waltke, *Theological Wordbook of the Old Testament*, Vol. 2 (Chicago: Moody Press, 1980), p. 958, #2472.

2. James Strong, *Strong's Exhaustive Concordance of the Bible* (Peabody, MA: Henrickson Publishers, n.d.), #H8334, **Sharath**.

Chapter Six

Confronting the Control Spirit

The Jezebel spirit is essentially a demonic control spirit that seeks to dominate by whatever means necessary. When allowed to prevail, it aborts the birthing of those things that the Lord wants to bring forth both in the lives of His people and in the nations of the earth. It is seductive and enticing on the surface, promising much but delivering nothing. "For the lips of an adulteress drip honey, and smoother than oil is her speech; but in the end she is bitter as wormwood, sharp as a two-edged sword. Her feet go down to death, her steps take hold of Sheol" (Prov. 5:3-5).

Like the adulteress in these verses, the Jezebel spirit is spiritual harlotry masquerading as genuine intimacy. Its outward appearance of vibrant life and fruitfulness hides an inner barrenness. Those who are drawn in are led to their destruction. The Jezebel spirit sidles up to its victims cooing with soothing words of false comfort, then suddenly slashes and cuts them to pieces with bared fangs and claws.

In order to successfully confront and defeat this menace, the Church must first learn to recognize it for what it is. Believers must know how to identify its presence and effects within their own midst before pointing it out in others. They must remove the plank from their own eye before trying to remove the speck from someone else's eye. This is especially true when preparing to deal with this manipulative, controlling spirit that is so deeply entrenched in American, European, and other societies.

Identifying a Jezebel spirit requires discernment and discretion and must be handled with great care. Too many Christians have had their spirits crushed and their ministries damaged because an insensitive brother or sister falsely and carelessly accused them of being under a control spirit or being a "Jezebel." Let us again emphasize for clarity's sake— demonic spirits do not have gender! Secondly, some people, both men and women, have strong personalities and strong leadership abilities. But this does not mean they are operating under the influence of a "control spirit." And thirdly, your pastor is not your enemy; your pastor is your friend!

RECOGNIZING A JEZEBEL SPIRIT

The Jezebel spirit doggedly pursues its own divisive and destructive agenda, absolutely intent on getting its own way. Although subtle in its ways, this spirit is not invisible. Certain characteristics commonly appear whenever a Jezebel spirit is at work. These symptoms do not automatically mean that such a spirit is present, but they should serve as warning signals to alert believers. Again, careful and prayerful discernment is called for.

1.   The ultimate goal of a Jezebel spirit is always *control*. Every thought, every stratagem, every effort is directed at usurping another and taking over. Usually, the preferred method is a very subtle and low-key approach, at least in the beginning.

2. Because its goal is control, a Jezebel spirit takes aim especially at persons in authority: spouse, pastor, elders, boss, or anyone else in leadership. It does this to create a vacuum that it wants to fill.

3. A Jezebel spirit stirs up fear, flight, and discouragement, often prompting a spiritual leader to flee his or her appointed place just as Elijah did. Every year hundreds of spiritual marketplace and governmental leaders resign because of debilitating discouragement, confusion, depression, loss of vision, despair, disorientation, withdrawal, a sense of worthlessness, defeat, burnout, physical illness, financial insufficiency, character assassination, moral failure, and an almost infinite variety of other factors. In many cases, this maligning control spirit is responsible.

4. People under a Jezebel spirit often are naturally born leaders who have come under another influence instructing them how to operate covertly. Many of them actually have a leadership call on their life, but because they have never surrendered the issue of their personal ambition, that call becomes distorted. Therefore a mixture occurs. They seek to advance their own purposes by gaining the ear and the trust of influential people whom they can use in their climb to the top.

5. People who are insecure and wounded and who have pronounced ego needs are particularly susceptible to this seductive, manipulative spirit. Trying to fill a love deficit in their lives, they seek constant affirmation and approval. They crave popularity. They need to be needed, to be on the "inside track" and therefore make others dependent on them. In many cases they may have experienced rejection or abandonment at some point,

creating fear, insecurity, an obsession with self-preservation, resistance to authority, and bitterness.

6. A Jezebel spirit operates deceptively and with extreme subtlety. Its seeds of manipulation and control are cleverly disguised as flattery, encouragement, affirmation, and sometimes even wise counsel. Once planted, however, they grow quickly into weeds of destruction. Flattery will get you nowhere!

7. No one under this influence can operate effectively and unchallenged without an "Ahab" present. This spirit always tries to attach itself to a leader who is weak in character, someone who is powerful but pliable.

8. Ultimately, a Jezebel spirit is always in alignment with a "religious" and/or a "political" spirit. It operates behind a façade of decency, orthodoxy, and pious devotion. It might even demand the strictest of outward obedience.

9. Quite often, the natural family where this spirit operates is out of order. Chaos, confusion, and division rule the day. Rebellion is the seed Jezebel plants in the next generation.

RECKONING WITH A JEZEBEL SPIRIT

Once this controlling spirit has been identified, there are several important principles to follow in dealing with it effectively.

1. Be stable. Stability is one of the fundamental weapons of spiritual warfare. The issue is not maturity as much as being securely planted, firmly rooted in Christ. Those who hope in Christ are stable

because He is an anchor that holds firm, immovable and unshakeable amidst any storm. "This hope we have as an anchor of the soul, a hope both sure and steadfast and one which enters within the veil, where Jesus has entered as a forerunner for us, having become a high priest forever according to the order of Melchizedek" (Heb. 6:19-20). Stay attached to the Solid Rock. Don't be swayed!

2. Don't "check out." When the going gets tough, it is easy to feel like giving up and saying, "I'm tired. I think I'll just sit this one out." Don't do it! That's when vulnerability is the highest. A "check out" mentality opens the door for the enemy to send in deceptive words of false comfort. Stay engaged with faith. Don't run away from godly authority and accountability; instead, run *to* them. This is not the time to avoid the fellowship of other believers. Don't check out; check in!

3. Be ruthless in your own life in dealing with the desire to control, even when it comes because of fear and hurt. The desire to control circumstances to avoid being hurt again is another form of checking out. Release that desire to God and let Him replace it with peace and assurance. Seek healing and walk in the light.

4. Allow Jesus to take His rightful place as Lord and Master instead of letting other people fill that void. Human relationships of friends and family are important, but ultimately God is the only one who can fill the emotional and spiritual voids in each person's life. Don't look to receive from others that which only God can give. That is a lesson that takes a lifetime to learn. But learn it step by step.

5. Don't idolize people, especially their giftings. Gifts do not guard against human weaknesses and failings. Spiritual gifts are no protection against an "Achilles' heel." Only the eyes of God offer protection. Do this by walking with others who will watch your "backside."

In the final analysis, the biggest secret to dealing with the control spirit is learning how to yield to God and trust in Him; learning how to "let go and let God." Anything released to God He will return greatly multiplied. This principle is clearly illustrated in the lives of two remarkable women of the Bible, Hannah and Mary, and one man of extraordinary faith, the patriarch Abraham. So in our journey of discovering Elijah's Revolution, let's take a glance at the lives of these three.

SAMUEL—THE PRAYER CHILD

*S*amuel was a priest who also served as the last judge in Israel. As such he was a pivotal figure in Israel's transition from judges to kings. From a very early age, even before he knew God, Samuel's heart was inclined toward Him.

Now the boy Samuel was ministering to the Lord before Eli. And word from the Lord was rare in those days, visions were infrequent. And it happened at that time as Eli was lying down in his place (now his eyesight had begun to grow dim and he could not see well), and the lamp of God had not yet gone out, and Samuel was lying down in the temple of the Lord where the ark of God was, that the Lord called Samuel; and he said, "Here I am." Then he ran to Eli and said, "Here I am, for you called me." But he said, "I did not call, lie down again." So he went and lay down. And the Lord called yet again, "Samuel!" So Samuel arose and went to Eli, and said, "Here I am, for you called me." But he answered, "I did not call, my son, lie down again." Now Samuel did not yet know the Lord, nor had the word of the Lord yet been revealed to him. So the Lord called Samuel again for the third time. And he arose and went to Eli, and said, "Here I am, for you called me." Then Eli discerned that the Lord was calling the boy. And Eli said to Samuel, "Go lie down, and it shall be if He calls you, that you shall say, 'Speak, Lord, for Thy servant is listening.' " So Samuel went and lay down in his place. Then the Lord came and stood and called as at other times, "Samuel! Samuel!" And Samuel said, "Speak, for Thy servant is listening" (1 Samuel 3:1-10).

Samuel was born during a dry time in the spiritual life of Israel. Word from the Lord was rare and visions were infrequent. The "lamp of God" (symbolic of God's presence) "had not yet gone out." It was dim, but still burning.

Things had not always been this way. Eli, the old priest, had known the voice of the Lord, and in his days God's lamp had burned brightly. Now, however, sin had entered into the next generation. Eli's sons were also priests, but they did not walk in the footsteps of their father. They were corrupt, dishonest, and immoral, engaging in ritual prostitution at the very threshold of God's house. For some reason, Eli had failed to transfer the example of his godly leadership to his sons.

Even in the midst of man's unfaithfulness, God demonstrated His own faithfulness. In spite of rebellion and immorality, the lamp was still lit. Then there was Samuel. This little boy of the youngest generation was "lying down in the temple...where the ark of God was." The ark of God symbolized His presence and contained the Ten Commandments, Aaron's staff that budded, and a pot of manna. These items represented, respectively, the law of God, the authority of God, and the provision of God. Even though he did not yet know the Lord, Samuel had a desire to be where the Lord was. Shouldn't you also rest around the ark?

Where did Samuel get this desire? Certainly, God put it there, because He had plans for Samuel. More than that, however, Samuel's "God-wardness" was a legacy from his mother, Hannah. He too was a product of the joining of the generations.

Hannah was one of two wives of a man named Elkanah. Although she was the more loved of the two, Hannah had no children while Elkanah's other wife gave him many. Hannah's inability to have children caused her deep distress. One time while she was in Shiloh, near the house of the Lord, she cried out to God out of her sorrow and pain.

> *And she made a vow and said, "O Lord of hosts, if Thou wilt indeed look on the affliction of Thy maidservant and remember me, and not forget Thy maidservant, but wilt give Thy maidservant a son, then I will give him to the Lord all the days of his life, and a razor shall never come on his head"* (1 Samuel 1:11).

Hannah promised God that if He gave her a son she would dedicate him back to God as a lifelong Nazirite! The Lord honored Hannah and answered her prayer.

> *And Elkanah had relations with Hannah his wife, and the Lord remembered her. And it came about in due time, after Hannah had conceived, that she gave birth to a son; and she named him Samuel, saying, "Because I have asked him of the Lord"* (1 Samuel 1:19b-20).

That's what the name *Samuel* means: "asked of the Lord." A modern paraphrase would be "prayer child." Samuel was Hannah's "prayer child." She had asked God for him, and God had given him to her.

This is where Hannah faced her greatest challenge. Making a promise to God was one thing; following through with it was another. Samuel's birth tested Hannah at a whole new level. She had to deal with the issue of control. After Samuel was born, it would have been very natural for Hannah to cling to him, to clutch tightly to her precious child and never let him go. To do so would break her promise to God. Worse still, it would prevent Samuel from fulfilling his destiny in the Lord.

Hannah passed the test. She honored her promise to God just as He had honored her prayer for a son. Hannah let go and released Samuel into God's service. After she weaned him, she took him to Eli and said, "For this boy I prayed, and the Lord has given me my petition which I asked of Him. So I have also dedicated him to the Lord; as long as he lives he is dedicated to the Lord" (1 Sam. 1:27-28a). From that day Eli took Samuel and began to teach him and train him in the priestly service.

Hannah could have held onto Samuel, but she knew that whatever she released to God He would return to her greatly multiplied. Under Hannah's care, Samuel could have grown up to be a good man and a faithful follower of God. Because his mother dedicated him to the Lord, however, Samuel became much more than that. He became not only a judge, a priest, and a prophet, but also the *anointer* of kings and prophets. Because of Hannah's faithfulness, Samuel became a hinge of history for his people in his day. Hannah passed the test. Will you?

HIS FATHER'S BUSINESS

Probably no one who has ever walked the face of the earth has faced a greater test of the control spirit than did Mary, the mother of Jesus. Entrusted with the awesome responsibility and privilege of caring for and raising the Son of God, young Mary faced daily challenges. One of the strongest of these, very likely, was a sense of possessiveness. After all, she gave birth to Jesus, the long-awaited Messiah. She changed His diapers, wiped His nose, soothed His cuts and scrapes, taught Him His Hebrew and Aramaic. Like any good mother, Mary invested a lot of time, energy, and attention to Jesus. He was her son—her baby boy.

At the same time, Mary knew Jesus was unique. As the Son of God conceived in her by the Holy Spirit, Jesus was very different from Mary's other children, the natural products of her union with Joseph, who came later. It was probably quite a challenge for Mary and Joseph to strike a proper balance between remembering Jesus' unique nature and yet not playing favorites within the family. Talk about a test!

One of the first real tests of control that Mary and Joseph faced was in Jesus' twelfth year, during their annual pilgrimage to Jerusalem. When Mary and Joseph started for home, Jesus, unknown to them, remained behind. After returning to Jerusalem and searching for three days, the frantic parents found Jesus sitting calmly in the temple complex, listening to the teachers and asking them questions. Mary's honest question brought from her son a response that challenged all her maternal instincts for control.

> *And when they saw Him, they were astonished; and His mother said to Him, "Son, why have You treated us this way? Behold, Your father and I have been anxiously looking for You." And He said to them, "Why is it that you were looking for Me? Did you not know that I had to be in My Father's house?" (Luke 2:48-49)*

The King James Version translates Jesus' words as, "How is it that ye sought Me? wist ye not that I must be about *My Father's business?*" Imagine how Jesus' words must have cut straight to the hearts of Mary and Joseph! Already at the age of 12, the age for His *bar mitzvah*, the coming-of-age rite for Jewish males in which they are regarded as men and spiritually responsible for their decisions, Jesus knew who He was and what He was to do. He understood that His destiny lay beyond the comforts of home and the confines of Nazareth and Joseph's carpenter shop.

Jesus' earthly parents had to recognize that their son had a heavenly Father who had a higher claim upon Him, who was jealous for Him to fulfill His divine purpose and destiny. Mary and Joseph faced the challenge of trusting God and letting Jesus go.

As the days went by, Mary, still relatively a young woman, faced other similar tests. Once, when Jesus was informed that His mother and brothers wanted to see Him, He said, " 'Who is My mother and who are My brothers?' And stretching out His hand toward His disciples, He said, 'Behold, My mother and My brothers! For whoever shall do the will of My Father who is in heaven, he is My brother and sister and mother' " (Mt. 12:48b-50). Jesus was not ignoring or denying His human family ties. He was stating that certain fundamental changes had occurred in His relational priorities. Because of His redemptive mission that was leading Him to the cross, Jesus' outward relationship with His family would be forever different.

Jesus never forsook His responsibilities as the eldest son. At some point along the way, apparently, Joseph died. He does not appear any more after Luke's account of the trip to Jerusalem when Jesus was 12. As the eldest son, Jesus would have become head of the household upon Joseph's death, and the welfare of His mother was His responsibility. Jesus discharged this responsibility even from the cross when He committed Mary into the care of "the disciple whom He loved," probably John (see Jn. 19:26-27).

Not that she could have done anything to stop it, Jesus' crucifixion was Mary's greatest test in the area of control. She had to face the reality of giving away—forever as far as she knew—that which God had given to her in the greatest one-time act in all of history. God had given Jesus to her, and she had to give Him back. Mary passed the ultimate test because she understood that God had given Jesus not only to her, but also to the world. Only by willingly giving Him up could she watch Him fulfill His destiny as the Lamb of God who takes away the sin of the world and as the King of kings who reigns forever as the risen Lord. So it also is with all parents—the ultimate test is to yield your precious heirs into the hands of another. This is one of the greatest tests in all life—to yield the right of way.

ISAAC—THE PROMISE CHILD

In many ways, the entire life of Abraham is a picture of what it means to confront the control spirit and learn to continually yield it to the Lord. Abraham learned to trust God and believe His promises even when outward circumstances suggested otherwise. First, God directed him to leave his home and country and go to a country that God would show to Him. (Did you know that transition is never easy?) Second, God promised Abraham a son of his own, even though he and his wife, Sarah, were too old to have children.

> *By faith Abraham, when he was called, obeyed by going out to a place which he was to receive for an inheritance; and he went out, not knowing where he was going. By faith he lived as an alien in the land of promise, as in a foreign land, dwelling in tents with Isaac and Jacob, fellow-heirs of the same promise; for he was looking for the city which has foundations, whose architect and builder is God. By faith even Sarah herself received ability to conceive, even beyond the proper time of life, since she considered Him faithful who had promised; therefore, also, there was born of one man, and him as good as dead at that, as many descendants as the stars of heaven in number, and innumerable as the sand which is by the seashore* (Hebrews 11:8-12).

Twenty-five years passed between God's promise of a son to Abraham and its fulfillment. During that time Abraham faced tests both of faith and control. At one point he tried to help God out by having a son by Hagar, Sarah's handmaid.

Although God blessed that son, Ishmael, and made him fruitful, Ishmael was not the promise child. Finally, when Abraham was 100 years old and Sarah 99, Isaac was born.

Although Abraham had learned much during a century of life and was a great man of faith, his biggest test still lay ahead. Some years later, God commanded Abraham to take Isaac, his precious promise child, and offer him as a burnt offering. The Bible does not record what thoughts went through Abraham's mind or what struggles he had with the control issue. It simply records that he obeyed. But can you just imagine the intensity of inner turmoil and mental anguish Abraham probably went through?

> *By faith Abraham, when he was tested, offered up Isaac; and he who had received the promises was offering up his only begotten son; it was he to whom it was said, "In Isaac your descendants shall be called." He considered that God is able to raise men even from the dead; from which he also received him back as a type* (Hebrews 11:17-19).

Of course, God stopped Abraham before he slew his son and provided a ram for the sacrifice instead. Abraham's obedience proved that he trusted God in all things and valued Him higher than anyone or anything else. Abraham passed his greatest test, and as a result he fathered a nation of people through whom the entire world was blessed. It was through Abraham's descendants, the nation of Israel, that the Messiah, Jesus Christ, the Savior, came into the world. Now that's investing in the generations!

LOSING CONTROL

Ultimately, dealing with the control spirit has to do with recognizing the jealousy that God has toward the lives of each of His children. His desire is that His people be completely free from it, but that rarely happens all at once. Deliverance from the control spirit occurs progressively through the consecutive stages of life. New levels bring new tests. Through it all, the Lord gently and patiently guides, helping those whose hearts are turned toward Him learn to let go of the things and the attitudes that they are trying to control, but which in reality control them.

Part of the heart issue that the Lord is after is to cleanse and remove from His people their obsession with controlling and managing that which they birth. That's human nature, but human nature stands in opposition to God. If you do not pass this test, then that may become an access point where "possessiveness" will lead to even darker paths where Jezebel tends to dwell.

Many people are deathly afraid of losing control of their lives. They feel secure only when they can manage every penny, every detail, and every circumstance. Psychiatric wards are filled with people who have tried and failed. It is only in losing control by willingly releasing it to God that anyone can experience life in its fullest abundance. Losing control to God is liberating because it frees one to focus on living and following the will of God while leaving the details to Him.

Only by releasing our stewardship to Him can promises be returned greatly multiplied. How many times throughout the history of the Church have individuals or congregations missed the fullness of what God wanted to do in and through them because they would not trust Him with their hopes, their dreams, and their resources?

The Bible calls this walking by faith. Abraham lived his entire life this way. Two characteristic attitudes of someone who is walking by faith are flexibility and a sense of always being in motion—always on a journey with the final destination still to come. Abraham went where God led him because he was not looking just for land or a home, but for a "city...whose architect and builder is God" (Heb. 11:10b). Abraham was not after a *place*—he was after the builder of the place! Life was the journey; God was the destination.

MOVING FORWARD INTO THE UNKNOWN

Flexibility requires humility, because it involves accepting the fact that a life of faith means not always understanding everything or seeing the complete picture at the beginning. Sometimes God's instructions won't make any sense from a strictly human point of view. In fact, they may sound downright foolish. God's purpose in giving such instructions to His children is to set them in motion, to get them to let go of the controls of their lives and start moving toward the destiny He has planned for them.

Being in motion means being less in control. It means getting out of the "unholy comfort zone" and onto the cutting edge of life, and that is walking by faith. It may mean leaving a six-figure income and a "secure" future in order to work with ghetto children or the people of a third-world country. It may mean following God to a new place only to have the end result be completely different from what was expected. It may mean simply learning to live each day with a lighter grip on things and circumstances and "casting all your anxiety upon Him, because He cares for you" (1 Pet. 5:7).

It might mean fasting, sacrificing, and praying like never before. It might mean hearing a word to launch The Call to the Mall and not having a dime to start it. Whatever the case, losing control will cause you to propel forward in a spirit of faith.

Walking by faith, or letting go of the control spirit, means being willing for God to change the road map of life from time to time and draw in an alternate route. Wherever

He leads, one thing is certain: He is preparing to birth something wonderful and beyond imagination, something that simply cannot and will not happen unless He is in control.

It's easy to dream; it's another thing entirely to walk out that dream. In the same way, it's easy to profess faith in God, but walking that faith is another matter altogether. Samuel learned at an early age to say, "Speak, Lord, for Your servant is listening." A submissive heart that is willing to listen is a critical key to hearing God's voice. Both of us being fathers of families, we know one of the first things you attempt to teach your children is to listen and obey.

The ability to listen—to really hear—is tied to the inner condition of the heart. Only a heart inclined toward God will hear Him. An inclined heart that hears God will listen to Him. This is the essence of obedience. The only people who really hear God in the first place are those who stand ready to obey Him. Those who are obedient will listen, and those who listen will hear, and those who hear will do.

Don't be afraid to let go of the controls. God is perfectly capable of managing things. In fact, He is the only one who can do it right. Don't hold on so tightly! Let go and let God! Go ahead, lose control![1] Combat Jezebel's influence to dominate and control everything and walk in an opposite spirit of the Kingdom of God by yielding to His right of way.

ENDNOTE

1. By "losing control," we are not referring to walking in an independent rebellious manner. After all, the fruit of the Spirit is "self-control." Self-control deals with the way you handle anger, appetites, and the lusts of the flesh. But we are not to "control" the Holy Spirit. He is to control us. So by using the term "losing control" we are using a form of contemporary language meaning to yield your rights to God.

Part Three

A Time for Sacrifice

Chapter Seven

The Esther Mandate

One of the young people who took the lead during *The Call DC* was a 14-year-old girl who had been praying every day for a year for God to reverse *Roe v. Wade* and to bring prayer back into the schools. At one point she stood on the platform with microphone in hand and prayed, "God, release the Esther anointing. Change *Roe v. Wade*. Break the demonic decrees off of this land!"

God honors prayers like that. This young lady was from Kansas City. When the national touring team for *The Call* held a meeting at a church in Kansas City, she attended. Before leaving for the meeting, she had felt a strange unction to paint stars on her feet. The name *Esther* means "star."

She painted stars on her toes and on her feet, with diamonds in the middle of them, just because she felt that's what God wanted her to do. It was a warm night, so she wore sandals to the meeting. Unknown to her, another woman was at the meeting who had come from many miles away because of a word she received from God. The Lord had told her, "You will see a girl there tonight who has the anointing of Esther on her life, and you are to prophesy over her and bless her. You will know her by what is painted on her feet." Imagine that young lady's surprise when this woman, a complete stranger, walked up and began to prophesy over her!

There was more to this than just her calling. As that young lady prayed on the platform that day, having prepared herself, like Esther, with "beauty treatments" for a year, she stood as a representational individual for the whole nation. She appealed to the Lord for the releasing of the Esther anointing— a season of fasting and prayer—for God to turn the nation and spare the people of America from His judgment.

In the Old Testament book that bears her name, Esther called a three-day fast for the breaking of a demonic decree that threatened the very survival of her people. A teenage Jewish orphan who was raised by her older cousin Mordecai, Esther became by God's design wife and queen to the king of the Persian Empire. This placed her in a perfect position to secure deliverance for the rest of the Jews in the land. At the right time, complete reversal came. Haman, chief minister to the king and the architect of the plan to destroy the Jews, was himself destroyed, and Mordecai was elevated to take his place. Esther came to the kingdom for just such an hour, and because she was faithful to her call, a nation was preserved.

God can do the same thing in America today. A teenager's fast changed history then and can change it now, because God is the same yesterday, today, and forever.

Prepared in Advance

Even though it never mentions Him by name, the Book of Esther is all about the sovereignty of God. The events depicted take place late in the Old Testament history of the Jews. It is after the Babylonian captivity, and many Jews, stirred by a prophetic spirit and a longing for home, have already returned to Palestine with Ezra and Nehemiah.

The Temple in Jerusalem has been rebuilt and the walls of the city repaired. Esther is a story about the Jews who did *not* return, but who remained in Persia. Many of these were secular Jews, content to live in a Gentile land and assimilate much of its culture.

The Jews who returned from Babylon to rebuild the Temple and reoccupy the promised land needed the assurance of knowing that God was with them. He reassured them through the prophet Haggai: "Then Haggai, the messenger of the Lord, spoke by the commission of the Lord to the people saying, ' "I am with you," declares the Lord' " (Hag. 1:13).

Although they remained behind, the Jews still in exile undoubtedly asked a similar question: "Are we still God's people?" The Book of Esther answers with a resounding "Yes!" Even those Jews who did not move with God's prophetic purposes were still under His covenant of love.

Nothing takes God by surprise. Years before the threat to Esther and her people even arose, God was already preparing for their deliverance.

It all began when King Ahasuerus threw a great banquet for all the nobles, military leaders, and attendants in his realm. Food was plentiful, wine flowed freely, and the king showed off his wealth and opulence. The celebration lasted for six months. Afterwards, the king gave another banquet in the palace garden for all the people who worked in the palace, from the great to the small. This party lasted seven days.

On the seventh day, while the king was half drunk with wine, he commanded his personal attendants to bring out Queen Vashti, wearing her royal crown, so he could show off her beauty to the people. When Vashti refused to come, the king was very angry and deposed her. All this took place during the third year of the king's reign.

Ahasuerus needed a new queen. Acting on the counsel of his attendants, he launched an empire-wide search for the most beautiful young virgins in the land, who would be brought into the king's harem. After a period of preparation, these young women would be brought before the king one by one, and whoever pleased him the most would become queen. The others would become the king's concubines, living the rest of their lives in luxury but also in loneliness, separated from their families and likely never again to be summoned into the king's presence.

One of the young virgins brought to the palace was Esther, who was "beautiful of form and face" (Esther 2:7). Her Hebrew name was Hadassah, which means "myrtle." After Esther was taken into the harem her cousin Mordecai, who had raised her as his own daughter after the deaths of her parents, checked on her welfare every day. On his instructions, Esther told no one in the palace that she was a Jew.

Initially, Esther may have felt that her future was dark. She may have asked, "Lord, why am I in this situation? Will I have to spend the rest of my life in the loneliness of the concubines' quarters?" Sometimes those days that appear darkest prove to be doors of destiny. It all depends on attitude. Esther may not have realized it at the time, but God was preparing her for a divine destiny, placing her in a strategic position in the kingdom of Persia to meet a specific crisis.

The answer for dark days is not to grumble or complain, but to focus on God rather than on circumstances, looking for the door of destiny rather than the avenue of escape.

Whatever Esther's initial thoughts or feelings may have been, she nevertheless quickly impressed Hegai, the eunuch in charge of the women, who gave her favored treatment.

After a year of special beauty treatments, which was the standard preparation for women in the harem, Esther was ready to meet the king.

Ahasuerus was quite taken with her.

And the king loved Esther more than all the women, and she found favor and kindness with him more than all the virgins, so that he set the royal crown on her head and made her queen instead of Vashti. Then the king gave a great banquet, Esther's banquet, for all his princes and his servants; he also made a holiday for the provinces and gave gifts according to the king's bounty (Esther 2:17-18).

What captivated Ahasuerus about Esther was not just her physical beauty but the beauty of a quiet spirit, a spirit at rest in God. Esther trusted God to do with her what He would. She laid her life in the hands of a loving God who moved by divine providence to put her where He wanted her to be. Esther had a great calling on her life, and she had charisma. More than that, she had character, and character is what counts.

Four years had passed since Vashti was deposed as queen; five more were to pass before Haman hatched his plot to destroy the Jews. *Nine years in advance* God was already setting the stage to place Esther in position to fulfill her destiny of saving her people from destruction!

God is sovereign. He is always at work moving human events to serve His own divine purposes, that He might be glorified. The amazing thing is that He deliberately chooses and uses people in His plans.

IDENTITY CRISIS

At first, Esther may not have really known who she was. Was she Hadassah, a Jew and a child of God, or was she Esther, a child of the Persian culture? Although *Esther* means "star," it also may be a variation of the name *Ishtar*, a pagan goddess. Who was she?

Many young people in America face a similar identity crisis. They don't know who they are. One of the reasons is that the definition of truth has become so vague in modern American society. Josh McDowell, one of the leading Christian consultants and experts on youth culture in the country, says that Americans today live not in a Christian or post-Christian, but an *anti-Christian* culture. No longer is truth defined in terms of absolute values or clear-cut right and wrong. Instead, truth is relative. Truth is whatever anyone perceives it to be. Tragically, this relative concept of truth is very prevalent even among *Christian* young people. At one time, tolerance meant a willingness to accept someone who held different beliefs, but not any longer. Tolerance today says, "Not only is it okay for you to believe what you believe, it is *right* for you to believe it if that is what you want to believe. Truth is not absolute; truth is whatever is true for you." There is a big difference.

Like Esther, many of today's young people are orphans, spiritually speaking. This is a fatherless generation. They don't know who they are. The critical need of today's youth is that they discover their identity. "For this reason, I bow my knees before the Father, from whom every family in heaven and on earth derives its name" (Eph. 3:14-15). Identity comes from God the Father. He takes up the fatherless generation, and those who are committed to Him and carry His heart will do the same.

A DEMONIC PLOT

Sometime after Esther became queen, and with her help, Mordecai foiled a plot to assassinate the king.

Although the incident was recorded in the official chronicles of the kingdom, for some reason Mordecai never received any public recognition for his role in saving the king's life. After awhile it was forgotten.

Now it was time for Haman, the villain and archenemy of the story, to step onto the stage. When Haman entered the picture, Esther had been queen for five years. She still followed the counsel of Mordecai.

> *After these events King Ahasuerus promoted Haman, the son of Hammedatha the Agagite, and advanced him and established his authority over all the princes who were with him. And all the king's servants who were at the king's gate bowed down and paid homage to Haman; for so the king had commanded concerning him. But Mordecai neither bowed down nor paid homage* (Esther 3:1-2).

Haman was an Amalekite, a descendant of the king Agag. The Amalekites were a people who vigorously opposed Israel during the days of Moses, and God had declared war on them for all generations. God commanded Saul, Israel's first king, to totally annihilate the Amalekites. Saul's failure to do so was one of the reasons God replaced him as king, choosing David instead. As a result of Saul's disobedience, the Amalekites remained to harass and trouble the Jews for centuries.

Despite Haman's high position, Mordecai refused to bow and pay him homage. Perhaps it was because Mordecai, as a Jew, would bow and pay homage to God alone or perhaps because he recognized that Haman and his people were traditional and implacable enemies of the Jews. Whatever the reason, Mordecai's refusal filled Haman with rage. Haman's hatred was so intense that he was not satisfied with only killing Mordecai; he set out to kill every Jew in the kingdom.

First, Haman deceived Ahasuerus into believing that the Jews were a threat to the security of the kingdom. Then he obtained the king's permission to deal with the problem any way he wished. Haman's next step was to issue a decree in the king's name and sealed with the king's seal, ordering the annihilation of the Jews. "Letters were sent by couriers to all the king's provinces to destroy, to kill, and to annihilate all the Jews, both young and old, women and children, in one day, the thirteenth day of the twelfth month, which is the month Adar, and to seize their possessions as plunder" (Esther 3:13). This decree was issued 11 months in advance to give all the enemies of the Jews time to prepare for the slaughter.

Haman's decree was a demonic plot intent on destroying godly seed and heritage. Similar forces are busily at work in America today. What else could lie behind the moral and spiritual confusion and compromise that is so evident in every level of society? What else could explain governmental decisions making it legal to kill unborn babies and illegal to pray in school? What else could account for the government's stance that the laws of God have no place in American jurisprudence despite the fact that the Constitution of the United States is based on those very laws?

As in Esther's day, a demonic plot is afoot in America. A war to the death is underway, but most Americans are still sleeping. The Body of Christ in America needs to wake up before it is too late. The Elijah Revolution is one way that God is issuing a wake-up call. Many are responding, but many more are needed.

FASTING FOR DELIVERANCE

Sheltered as she was in the palace, Esther was at first unaware of Haman's sinister plans. Such was not the case with Mordecai and the rest of the Jews.

When Mordecai learned all that had been done, he tore his clothes, put on sackcloth and ashes, and went out into the midst of the city and wailed loudly and bitterly. And he went as far as the king's gate, for no one was to enter the king's gate clothed in sackcloth. And in each and every province where the command and decree of the king came, there was great mourning among the Jews, with fasting, weeping, and wailing; and many lay on sackcloth and ashes (Esther 4:1-3).

Although no mention is made of God, the actions described here are those of a people pouring their heart out to the Lord, imploring Him to rescue them. Their behavior reflects the fast called for in the Book of Joel:

"Yet even now," declares the Lord, "Return to Me with all your heart, and with fasting, weeping, and mourning; and rend your heart and not your garments." Now return to the Lord your God, for He is gracious and compassionate, slow to anger, abounding in lovingkindness, and relenting of evil. Who knows whether He will not turn and relent, and leave a blessing behind Him, even a grain offering and a libation for the Lord your God? Blow a trumpet in Zion, consecrate a fast, proclaim a solemn assembly" (Joel 2:12-15).

This is God's means of averting judgment or disaster in times of crisis. Calling His people to fasting, weeping, and mourning is God's way of turning things around.

When Esther learned of Mordecai's fasting and mourning, she asked him what was going on. He informed her of Haman's edict, provided her with a copy of it, and instructed her to appeal to the king on behalf of her people. Now Esther faced a great personal crisis. Under the laws of the kingdom, anyone, including the queen, who approached the king in his inner court without being summoned by him faced death. The only reprieve was if the king himself extended his scepter toward that person, thus granting the unscheduled audience. It had been a month since the king had last summoned Esther. If she took it upon herself to go to him, she could be killed. What was she to do?

Mordecai's response helped Esther make up her mind.

Then Mordecai told them to reply to Esther, "Do not imagine that you in the king's palace can escape any more than all the Jews. For if you remain silent at this time, relief and deliverance will arise for the Jews from another place and you and your father's house will perish. And who knows whether you have not attained royalty for such a time as this?" Then Esther told them to reply to Mordecai, "Go, assemble all the Jews who are found in Susa, and fast for me; do not eat or drink for three days, night or day. I and my maidens also will fast in the same way. And thus I will go in to the king, which is not according to the law; and if I perish, I perish" (Esther 4:13-16).

Esther had no doubts now as to who she was or where her destiny lay. She was Hadassah, a Jew and a child of God, and her destiny lay with her people. They were all in God's hands. Esther lived in luxury and enjoyed the pampered life of a queen, but she knew she could not hide there. The critical need of the hour called her to risk it all and step forward into her destiny, for better or for worse. Calling Mordecai and the Jews of the capital city to fast for three days along with her and her handmaidens, Esther resolved to go to the king. Esther's three-day fast turned the tide for her people and spelled the beginning of the end for Haman and his evil designs.

Today is not the time for the people of God to live for comfort. It's not the time to look for a hiding place or an escape route. The only hiding place is in Jesus; the only "escape" is into the arms of God, seeking His face and resolved to do His will. There is no other safe place.

Many Christians in America today simply seek to avoid pain or inconvenience at all costs. Regardless of what the future holds, no matter who is right or wrong concerning the details of Christ's return, one thing is clear: In the days ahead it is going to be harder to *live* for God than to *die* for Him. True martyrdom comes in living each day in faithful obedience to the Lord no matter what, saying no to sin and compromise and yes to God and holiness. This is not a time for silence. The hour has come for God's people to take a stand, to sacrifice themselves, like Esther, in fasting and prayer for the deliverance of a nation. Who knows but that God may turn the tide of history in America?

TURNING THE TIDE

Throughout the Book of Esther the unseen hand of God is behind the scenes guiding circumstances and people toward His own purposes. Proverbs 21:1 says, "The king's heart is like channels of water in the hand of the Lord; He turns it wherever He wishes." After her three-day fast, Esther prepared herself and went unbidden to see her husband, the king. God caused Ahasuerus to look favorably on Esther's unexpected appearance.

> *And it happened when the king saw Esther the queen standing in the court, she obtained favor in his sight; and the king extended to Esther the golden scepter which was in his hand. So Esther came near and touched the top of the scepter. Then the king said to her, "What is troubling you, Queen Esther? And what is your request? Even to half of the kingdom it will be given to you"* (Esther 5:2-3).

Esther had carefully thought out her strategy. Rather than just blurting everything out, she invited the king to a banquet she was preparing and told him that Haman was invited as well. At the banquet the king again asked Esther what she wanted. She responded by inviting both men back the following day for another banquet.

Haman left the first banquet very high in spirit. His good mood evaporated, however, when he saw Mordecai, who still refused to do homage to him. At the advice of his wife and friends, Haman built a gallows and planned to hang Mordecai on it after he had gotten the king's permission to do so.

That night the king could not sleep, and he ordered that the book of the chronicles of the kingdom be read to him. Some things never change. Even then, government documents were seen as a surefire cure for insomnia! During the reading, the king learned of Mordecai's service in thwarting the assassination plot and asked if anything had been done to honor him. The answer was no.

At that moment, Haman arrived in the king's court to request permission to hang Mordecai. Before Haman could make his request, the king asked him what he would do for a man the king wanted to honor. Thinking that the king planned to honor him, Haman said that the honoree should be paraded through the city on horseback, led by one of the royal princes, while decked out in one of the king's robes and wearing a crown. The king promptly commanded Haman to honor Mordecai in just such a manner. Haman was to lead the processional himself! For a man of Haman's ego, this was a crushing blow. It was another nail in his coffin.

Haman's humiliation was barely over when he was summoned to the second banquet. During the wine, the king once more asked Esther what she wanted. Esther chose this strategic moment to reveal to the king her Jewish heritage.

Then Queen Esther answered and said, "If I have found favor in your sight, O king, and if it please the king, let my life be given me as my petition, and my people as my request; for we have been sold, I and my people, to be destroyed, to be killed and to be annihilated. Now if we had only been sold as slaves, men and women, I would have remained silent, for the trouble would not be commensurate with the annoyance to the king." Then King Ahasuerus asked Queen Esther, "Who is he, and where is he, who would presume to do thus?" And Esther said, "A foe and an enemy, is this wicked Haman!" Then Haman became terrified before the king and queen (Esther 7:3-6).

While the king stalked out to the garden in anger, Haman stayed behind to beg Esther for his life. As Haman pleaded with Esther, he fell down on her couch. The king, returning from the garden, interpreted this as an assault on Esther. In short order, Haman was hanged on the very gallows that he had built for Mordecai. In turn, Mordecai was chosen by the king to replace Haman.

Haman's plot failed. The tables were turned. Although the laws of the Persians prevented a signed edict of the king from being rescinded, the king permitted the Jews in his realm to prepare to defend themselves. When the appointed day arrived for the pogrom, it was Haman's allies, the enemies of the Jews, who were destroyed.

The Jews commemorated their deliverance with a great victory celebration that is still observed today in the annual feast of Purim.

REVERSING DEMONIC DECREES

It's time for a reversal of demonic decrees in America. Can God reverse *Roe v. Wade,* which legalized abortion in America? What about *Engle v. Vitale,* which outlawed prayer in the schools, or *Stone v. Gramm,* which mandated the removal of the Ten Commandments from all public buildings and offices?

Why can't He, if He is the same yesterday, today, and for-ever? He turned the tide in Esther's day, and He can do it again today. God is still the God of the Bible, and He's not finished with America. He can change America's future if American Christians will pray and fast. That is the key. What would happen in America if millions of Christians, young and old, men and women, committed themselves to fasting, seeking God's face, and praying, "Lord, turn the tide in America! Remove these demonic decrees!"? What would hap-pen if they prayed for God to remove the unrighteous and raise up the righteous as He did with Haman and Mordecai?

The Book of Esther records six feasts, three at the begin-ning and three toward the end, with a fast in between. Many commentaries suggest that the turning point came when the king couldn't sleep and learned how Mordecai had saved his life. In reality, the fast was the turning point. Everything that happened afterwards hinged on the fast.

Throughout history, major turning points in God's deal-ings with humanity have always hinged on prayer and fasting. Scripture makes this abundantly clear. The same is true today. A new generation is appearing who will walk in radical aban-donment to Christ. The "Elijahs," "Elishas," and "Jehus" of America are arising who will boldly proclaim "No toleration!" for the sins of Jezebel in the land. The "Esthers" of America are arising, coming with fasting and prayer and a resolve to sacrifice themselves for the deliverance of their nation, no matter what the personal cost. These young people are ready to make a difference, ready to step forth believing God for the reversing of demonic decrees and the breaking of demonic strongholds in the land. They have not appeared by accident. On the contrary, these passionate children of the King have "attained royalty for such a time as this."

The Greatest Harvest

The greatest harvest in the history of America and the nations of the earth is coming. The old decrees of Haman are beginning to crumble. Now is not the time to be passive or disengaged, but to move with God, saying, "Lord, where do I fit in?" Christ is stirring up His Church, and now is the hour to hear His voice and move with Him.

Destiny is in the hands of God, not in the hands of government or even church leaders. Those who faithfully follow God's call, He will raise up in due time. Promotion comes from the Lord, not from men. So many believers are looking for a "royal position" out there somewhere, never realizing that their royal position is right under their noses. Royal position has nothing to do with "office," but everything to do with influence. The old adage is very true that says, "Bloom where you are planted." God does the planting. Those who are faithful in the sphere of influence God assigns them will be given a larger sphere.

God wants to turn the world upside down, and He is beginning with His own people. The call has gone out for the "Esther mandate"—the sacrifice of prayer and fasting for the reversal of demonic decrees and the salvation of a nation. God turns His people upside down in order to make a difference in their lives so that they can make a difference in the world. Answer the call. Rise to the challenge of the Esther mandate. Become a world-changer. "And who knows whether you have not attained royalty for such a time as this?"

Chapter Eight

A Passion for Jesus

One of the crying needs of the modern Church in America and the nations is to recapture a holy passion for Jesus. This is first a very individual personal matter. There cannot be a "corporate" passion for Christ until there are fiery individuals who are passionately in love with Him and then who come together and their sparks start a genuine fire. One torch ignites another until the fire of His love spreads so as to take over whatever is in its path.

Authentic passion for Jesus can be described in many different ways. Andrew Murray, the great South African preacher, teacher, writer, and man of God of a century ago, called it "absolute surrender." Others, particularly Christians of America's Deep South in the nineteenth century, liked to refer to it as "being seized by the power of a great affection." Many have explained their passion by saying they were "consumed by God" or "possessed by God." Whatever terminology is used, the meaning is the same: singular and exclusive love and devotion to the person of the Lord Jesus Christ.

For devout Jews, all-consuming love for God is the very core of faith: "You shall love the Lord your God with all your heart and with all your soul and with all your might" (Deut. 6:5). Jesus called this the "great and foremost commandment" (Mt. 22:38). To the apostle Paul, Christ was everything:

For to me, to live is Christ, and to die is gain (Philippians 1:21).

But whatever things were gain to me, those things I have counted as loss for the sake of Christ. More than that, I count all things to be loss in view of the surpassing value of knowing Christ Jesus my Lord, for whom I have suffered the loss of all things, and count them but rubbish in order that I may gain Christ (Philippians 3:7-8).

Simon Peter declared that all true believers are part of the unique people of God who are possessed by Him:

*But you are a chosen race, a royal priesthood, a holy nation, **a people for God's own possession**, that you may proclaim the excellencies of Him who has called you out of darkness into His marvelous light; for you once were not a people, but **now you are the people of God**; you had not received mercy, but now you have received mercy* (1 Peter 2:9-10).

GIDEON—CLOTHED BY GOD

Gideon was possessed by God, and it changed his life. When his encounter with God came he was threshing grain down in a winepress to hide it from marauding bands of Midianites. "The angel of the Lord appeared to him and said to him, 'The Lord is with you, O valiant warrior....Go in this your strength and deliver Israel from the hand of Midian. Have I not sent you?'" (Judg. 6:12,14b) Gideon did not feel like a valiant warrior. "He said to Him, 'O Lord, how shall I deliver Israel? Behold, my family is the least in Manasseh, and I am the youngest in my father's house'" (Judg. 6:15). The Lord reassured him. "But the Lord said to him, 'Surely I will be with you, and you shall defeat Midian as one man'" (Judg. 6:16).

Gideon still needed some more convincing before he was ready to step out and follow God's call. Twice he put out his famous fleece, asking for confirmation, and twice the Lord responded. Even then, Gideon's first act was cautious. Out of fear of his father's servants and under cover of night Gideon pulled down and destroyed the altar to Baal and the Asherah pole that belonged to his father. After this, however, Gideon's boldness grew because God fulfilled His promise to be with him: "But the Spirit of the Lord clothed Gideon with Himself and *took possession of him*, and he blew a trumpet, and [the clan of] Abiezer was gathered to him" (Judg. 6:34 AMP). From there Gideon proceeded to rout the entire Midianite army with only 300 men of his own. The Lord brought Gideon a great victory as he was clothed with a strength that only God can provide.

Gideon's reward for facing his fears and tearing down the high places was to be clothed in and possessed by the Spirit of God. No wonder Gideon changed! You would too!

It is the same in every generation. The people God uses are rarely special or extraordinary people; they are typically ordinary people who have encountered an extraordinary God. They have touched God and God has touched them, and their lives are forever changed. That should encourage each of us to realize that we too can be "history makers"—a part of the Elijah Revolution.

CONSUMED BY ZEAL FOR GOD

Members of today's "Elijah" generation and other believers who have a radical passion for Jesus are certainly in good company. The long road of Church history is well lit by the flames of saints whose lives burned with the inner fire of God. During His earthly incarnation even Jesus Himself, although He was God, was consumed with a jealous zeal for His Father. As in all other things, His example in this regard is a model for every believer.

The final week of Jesus' earthly life began with His triumphal entry into Jerusalem riding on a beast of burden. This in itself was a messianic act and the fulfillment of a prophecy in Zechariah: "Rejoice greatly, O daughter of Zion! Shout in triumph, O daughter of Jerusalem! Behold, your king is coming to you; He is just and endowed with salvation, humble, and mounted on a donkey, even on a colt, the foal of a donkey" (Zech. 9:9). People thronged to meet Him and threw palm branches on the road in front of Him, welcoming Him with cries of "Hosanna to the Son of David; Blessed is He who comes in the name of the Lord; Hosanna in the highest!" (Mt. 21:9b)

"Son of David" is a title that in Jesus' day was generally understood to refer to the Messiah. In applying it to Jesus the people were acknowledging Him as a descendant of King David and heir to David's throne. Jesus was the fulfillment of God's promise to David that his line would occupy the throne of Israel forever (see 2 Sam. 7:13).

After this acclamation by the people, "Jesus entered the temple and cast out all those who were buying and selling in the temple, and overturned the tables of the moneychangers and the seats of those who were selling doves. And He said to them, 'It is written, "My house shall be called a house of prayer"; but you are making it a robbers' den' " (Mt. 21:12-13). Many people, believers and nonbelievers alike, have found this a rather disturbing picture of Jesus. It certainly does not fit the image of the "sweet and gentle Savior." Did Jesus simply lose His temper or was there something deeper at work here? John provides some insight in his version of the incident when he observes that "His disciples remembered that it was written, 'Zeal for Thy house will consume me'" (Jn. 2:17), which refers to Psalm 69:9: "For zeal for Thy house has consumed me, and the reproaches of those who reproach Thee have fallen on me."

Jesus was very jealous for the name and reputation of His Father and for the honor of His house. The money-changers and dove sellers were running an officially sanctioned operation of graft, greed, and dishonesty. They cheated people by charging exorbitant prices to exchange standard currency into temple currency that was acceptable for offerings, and to provide "preapproved" animals for sacrifice to replace those that they found, often without just cause, blemished or otherwise unacceptable. By approving of this arrangement, from which they received "kickbacks," the priests and other religious leaders, those who were entrusted with representing God before the people, dishonored God's house and sullied His reputation. They were giving God a "bad rap"—a "bad name."

Consumed by zeal for God, as a Son jealous for the good name of His Father, Jesus "upset the apple cart" to restore His Father's house to its intended purpose: a place of prayer where people could come to meet God. Passion for God brooks no tolerance for evil of any kind, especially when it keeps people separated or distanced from Him.

"LIKE THE VERY BREATH OF GOD"

One way to describe revival is when an "open heaven" appears over a region. Before Heaven opens over a region, however, it first opens over a person or a group of people who have passionately and ceaselessly pursued the face of God. Historically, passionate prayer always precedes revival. When the Lord touches a person and opens Heaven above him, wherever he goes the radiant, preeminent presence of the Lord emanates, producing a holy "radiation" zone that zaps anyone who comes into the area (or around the person). Do you want to be a carrier of His great presence? Let the Glorious Intruder first invade your own ungodly comfort zones and then He will use you to open the heavens for others.

Charles Finney was such a man. Under the ministry of this great nineteenth-century evangelist over 500,000 people were converted to Christ, 100,000 or more in New York alone. It is a well-documented fact that once when he entered a factory to speak to the workers, many of them came under deep spiritual conviction by his mere presence in the place. Finney had a contagious passion for Jesus. There was an open heaven over him, and the lives of thousands were transformed.

What fueled Charles Finney's passion? What lit the fire of God in his spirit? There is no better description than his own:

> There was no fire, and no light, in the room; nevertheless it appeared to me as if it were perfectly light. As I went in and shut the door after me, it seemed as if I met the Lord Jesus Christ face to face. It did not occur to me then, nor did it for some time afterward, that it was wholly a mental state. On the contrary it seemed to me that I saw Him as I would see any other man. He said nothing, but looked at me in such a manner as to break me right down at his feet. I have always since regarded this as a most remarkable state of mind; for it seemed to me a reality, that He stood before me, and I fell down at his feet and poured out my soul to Him. I wept aloud like a child, and made such confessions as I could with my choked utterance. It seemed to me that I bathed His feet with my tears; and yet I had no distinct impression that I touched Him, that I recollect.

I must have continued in this state for a good while; but my mind was too much absorbed with the interview to recollect anything that I said. But I know, as soon as my mind became calm enough to break off from the interview, I returned to the front office, and found that the fire that I had made of large wood was nearly burned out. But as I turned and was about to take a seat by the fire, I received a mighty baptism of the Holy Ghost. Without any expectation of it, without ever having the thought in my mind that there was any such thing for me, without any recollection that I had ever heard the thing mentioned by any person in the world, the Holy Spirit descended upon me in a manner that seemed to go through me, body and soul. I could feel the impression, like a wave of electricity, going through and through me. Indeed it seemed to come in waves and waves of liquid love, for I could not express it in any other way. It seemed like the very breath of God. I can recollect distinctly that it seemed to fan me, like immense wings.

No words can express the wonderful love that was shed abroad in my heart. I wept aloud with joy and love; and I do not know but I should say, I literally bellowed out the unutterable gushings of my heart. These waves came over me, and over me, and over me, one after the other, until I recollect I cried out, "I shall die if these waves continue to pass over me." I said, "Lord, I cannot bear any more;" yet I had no fear of death.[1]

Charles Finney was experientially possessed by God. Is there any wonder, then, why he made such an impact for Christ wherever he went?

UNITAS FRATRUM

When Christian believers fix their passion and focus on the person of Jesus Christ, great things happen. In the early eighteenth century the Moravians, operating from Herrnhut, their village on the Saxon estate of Count Nicholas von Zinzendorf, launched the modern missionary movement. One of their mottoes was "No one works unless someone prays." To that end, they initiated a "prayer meeting" that lasted more than 100 years. For over a century, unceasing prayer went up from Herrnhut 24 hours a day, 7 days a week. They were committed "to win for the Lamb the rewards of His suffering." God greatly honored their faithfulness and passion.

One secret to the Moravians' success was their commitment to the concept they called *unitas fratrum*, or "unity of the brotherhood." Because they were made up of religious refugees, dissidents, and outcasts who had fled persecution, the Moravians came from diverse backgrounds. Although they differed among themselves in numerous doctrinal and theological points, they achieved a remarkable degree of unity. This was due to the fact that they decided to seek unity not in doctrine or theology but in the centrality of the person of Jesus Christ. Whatever their other differences, the Moravians shared in common passionate personal devotion to Christ.

> The group of believers who gathered at Herrnhut to pursue their dream of religious freedom were in much the same state as most Christians are today. They came from widely diverse religious backgrounds. During the first five years of their communal existence after the community's founding in 1722, they experienced bickering, dissension, and strife. They were no better or worse than you or I, but they made a deep commitment to Jesus Christ

and to prayer, which transformed and changed them forever. They began to think God-sized thoughts and feel a burning God-like compassion for the lost. They received supernatural faith to tackle challenges that would in many cases cost them their freedom or their very lives. Yet, they did it all in faithfulness and joy. The Moravians changed the world because they allowed God to change them. God wants to change the world again and He is looking at you and me. Are you willing to seek the same fire that inspired the Moravian believers two centuries ago?[2]

As with the Moravians, true spiritual unity is found always and only in the person of Jesus Christ. It will never be achieved through the counsel of men or the compromises of religion. Jesus Christ is the common denominator that will bring all of God's people into unity.

"LORD, BEND ME"

The Welsh Revival of 1904-05 was one of the most phenomenal moves of God in the twentieth century and part of a worldwide evangelical awakening. One of the human instruments that God used to great effect in this revival was Evan Roberts, a young coal miner in his 20's. Roberts had been praying for revival in Wales since his teens. When he was 13, he asked an elder in his town, "When God comes, where does He show up?" The elder, who had witnessed divine visitations before, replied, "When God comes, He always shows up first at a prayer meeting." Roberts then began attending every prayer meeting he could. It didn't matter what denomination, what "label" the church wore; if they were praying he wanted to be there, because he wanted to be present when God showed up. Even at this young age, Evan Roberts had a passion for Jesus.

Roberts' role in the Welsh Revival began when, while a student at a Methodist academy, he attended a series of meetings led by Seth Joshua, a Presbyterian evangelist whose preaching was one of the catalysts of the revival. Geoff Waugh, a modern revival historian, describes what happened:

> There Seth Joshua closed his ministry on the Thursday morning crying out in Welsh, "Lord, bend us." Evan Roberts went to the front, kneeling and fervently praying "Lord, bend me"...Before entering the Academy he had a deep encounter with God and had a vision of all Wales being lifted up to heaven. After this he regularly slept lightly till 1 am, woke for hours of communion with God, and then returned to sleep. He was convinced revival would touch all Wales and eventually led a small band all over the country praying and preaching.
>
> In October 1904 in his first year at the Academy, after the impact of the Spirit on him at Seth Joshua's meetings, he took leave to return home to challenge his friends, especially the young people.
>
> The Spirit of God convicted people as Evan Roberts insisted:
>
> 1. You must put away any unconfessed sin.
>
> 2. You must put away any doubtful habit.
>
> 3. You must obey the Spirit promptly.
>
> 4. You must confess Christ publicly.
>
> He believed that a baptism in the Spirit was the essence of revival and that the primary condition of revival is that individuals should experience such a baptism in the Spirit.
>
> Evan Roberts travelled the Welsh valleys, often never preaching but sitting head-in-hands earnestly

praying. In Neath he spent a week in prayer without leaving his rooms. The revival packed the churches out, but no one saw him all that week. He paid a price in prayer and tears.[3]

Evan Roberts would not understand the modern American "quick fix" approach to Christianity that hopes to change the world with a daily five-minute devotional and two-minute prayer. Is it any wonder why so few American Christians have ever witnessed a mighty move of God or experienced a significant touch from Him? Christians of the "Elijah" generation are beginning to rediscover the inner fire that drove Evan Roberts, a fierce and fervent passion for Jesus that seeks nothing less than an all-out invasion of the Spirit of God across the land.

"THE LORD'S SERVANT WAS POSSESSED BY GOD"

Rees Howells was a powerful man of prayer, an intercessor. In the eyes of many people then and now, his prayers during World War II were a major factor in keeping Great Britain free from invasion by Nazi Germany.

Some time ago, when Jim was in Wales, God supernaturally opened a door and gave him an opportunity to meet with Rees Howells' son. Eighty-six years old at the time, Mr. Samuels was a rather reclusive person. He never gave interviews and rarely met with or prayed for people on a one-to-one basis. Jim remembers that day very well.

> I had been crying out to the Lord, saying, "Oh God, we need this kind of authority, and revelation, and intercession." The Lord heard the ache that was in my heart, and divinely set an appointment. Now my friend Sue and I were in the very same building, adjacent to the very same blue room where Rees Howells held many of his prayer meetings during

World War II. We were sitting in a room with his son, having British tea, very proper.

I asked Mr. Samuels, "Sir, how is it that your father, Mr. Howells, got the revelation of what to pray for when?" I knew he had not gotten it from the radio or by reading newspapers. "How did he know what battles to pray through where?"

Mr. Samuels answered, "Don't you think it's time for another crumpet?"

We chatted about many things, such as how over fifty years before they had received revelation and prophecies concerning the exodus of the Jews and had prayed through the prophecies of Jeremiah.

I felt that I had to try again. Respectfully and with the fear of God upon me I asked a second time, "Mr. Samuels, how did your father get revelation to know what to pray for when?"

He said to me, "Don't you think it's time for a little more tea?"

We continued to talk about other things until I felt that I couldn't stand it anymore; the raging bull was rising. So I asked once again, "Mr Samuels, how did your father get this revelation?"

My friend Sue was worse off than I was. She got on her knees right in front of him and gently said, "Mr. Samuels, our nation is in a time of need. We need this kind of revelation, and this kind of authority."

I asked him again, "Mr Samuels, how is it that your father and those with whom he prayed got this kind of revelation and authority? Did an angel come? Did it come by dreams or visions? How did this revelation come?"

Mr. Samuels saw that we were not going to leave without an answer. He looked at us, and with a tear trickling down his cheek said, "You must understand, the Lord's servant was possessed by God."

I didn't ask another question. I didn't have to; they had all been answered. I don't care if it was from an angel, I don't care if it was by dreams or visions, I don't care whether it was the confirmation of many voices. Revelation came because someone had touched God, and God had touched him. Someone had laid hold of the hem of His garment, and drawn forth His presence.

Mr. Samuels then did something wonderful. He laid his hands on us and prayed a very simple prayer, asking for the Father's blessing and for the anointing of crisis intervention through intercession to be passed on to the next generation. This was powerful confirmation for me, because some time before the Lord had already revealed to me that praying for crisis intervention was my next "assignment."

What is the key to revelation? What is the key to the prophetic? What is the key to moving in spiritual power? Very simply, the key to all these things is to be possessed by God.

PASSION FOR JESUS FUELS PREVAILING PRAYER

Radical prayer always precedes revival; this is an indisputable fact. Passionate love for Jesus leads to passionate prayer. What's so beautiful about this is that any believer can do it. Spiritual power and effectiveness are not limited to a special few or a corps of godly "elites." Any believer who chooses to love the Lord above all else and to believe His promises can know Him intimately and experience prevailing prayer. Age or physical condition have nothing to do with it. It is a matter of the heart.

After the horrors and struggle of World War II, spiritual life in many parts of the western world was at a very low point. A fresh touch from God was needed. This was as much true in the Scottish Hebrides as anywhere else. In 1949 two elderly sisters, Peggy and Christine Smith, began praying continually for revival. Peggy was 84 and blind; Christine, 82 and crippled with arthritis. As they prayed day after day they reminded God of His words in Isaiah:

> *The wilderness and the desert will be glad, and the Arabah will rejoice and blossom; like the crocus it will blossom profusely and rejoice with rejoicing and shout of joy. The glory of Lebanon will be given to it, the majesty of Carmel and Sharon. They will see the glory of the Lord, the majesty of our God.... Then the eyes of the blind will be opened, and the ears of the deaf will be unstopped. Then the lame will leap like a deer, and the tongue of the dumb will shout for joy. For waters will break forth in the wilderness and streams in the Arabah. And the scorched land will become a pool, and the thirsty ground springs of water* (Isaiah 35:1-2,5-7a).

Peggy and Christine prayed according to Isaiah 64:1a, "O that Thou wouldst rend the heavens and come down." He did. Revival historian Geoff Waugh relates how the Hebrides revival began:

God showed Peggy in a dream that revival was coming. Months later, early one winter's morning as the sisters were praying, God gave them an unshakable conviction that revival was near.

Peggy asked her minister, James Murray Mackay, to call the church leaders to prayer. Three nights a week, for several months, the leaders prayed together. One night, having begun to pray at 10 p.m., a young deacon from the Free Church read Psalm 24 and challenged everyone to be clean before God. As they waited on God, His awesome Presence swept over them in the barn at 4 a.m.

Mackay invited a man named Duncan Campbell to come and lead meetings. Within two weeks he came, despite having previous engagements. God had intervened and changed Duncan's plans and commitments. At the close of his first meeting in the Presbyterian church in Barvas, the travel-weary preacher received the invitation to join an all-night prayer meeting! Thirty people gathered for prayer in a nearby cottage.[4]

The Spirit of God fell that night and radiated out in every direction. All over the island men and women were seeking God and crying out for mercy and forgiveness, even people who were nowhere near the meetings! God was doing a completely supernatural work.

When Duncan Campbell and his friends arrived at the church that morning, it was already crowded. People had gathered from all over the island, some coming in buses and vans. No one discovered who told them to come. God led them. Large numbers were converted as God's Spirit convicted multitudes of sin, many lying prostrate, many weeping.[5]

Duncan Campbell's preaching continued for five weeks with the Lord working mightily in the hearts of many. Everywhere on the island people were experiencing the power and presence of God.

Although Duncan Campbell's name is written prominently in the history of the Hebrides revival, it was Peggy and Christine Smith in their home and a small group of faithful teenage boys in a barn who won through in prevailing prayer. (Sounds like the joining of the generations at work at that time as well.) At heart was their passion for Jesus and their burden to see the Lord's presence and power fall. They "plugged into" the divine power source. A "holy radiation zone" five miles wide fell from Heaven, all because God took possession of some people who believed that their little keys of prayer could open big doors.

He Can Do It Again!

God wants to do it again; He wants to send a revival. He is looking for people willing to pay the price in prevailing prayer and fasting. In this day and generation many are responding to His call. Believers of the "Elijah" generation are capturing the same spirit and passion for the Lord that illuminated and drove the lives of Gideon, Peter, Paul, Finney, the Moravians, Evan Roberts, Rees Howells, Peggy and Christine Smith, and Duncan Campbell. They are giving themselves over totally to be possessed by God, for Him to invade their unholy comfort zones and propel them into the places where He wants them to go.

The key is to be hungry and thirsty for Him. Jesus said, "Blessed are those who hunger and thirst for righteousness, for they shall be satisfied" (Mt. 5:6). The invitation in the Book of Revelation is "And the Spirit and the bride say, 'Come.' And let the one who hears say, 'Come.' And let the one who is thirsty come; let the one who wishes take the water of life without cost" (Rev. 22:17).

People with a passion for Jesus are perpetually thirsty for Him. Even as He fills them up with the water of life He whets their appetite for more. Passionate people are the ones God will use to change the world. Fence-sitters and the halfhearted rarely accomplish much. Those who have "signed on" for the Elijah Revolution are through with fence-sitting. They are through with halfhearted measures, whether theirs or someone else's. God's Spirit is moving. His army is growing. Revolutionaries are loose in the land preparing the way for revival through fasting and prevailing prayer. It happened before, and it can happen again. In the words of an old gospel hymn, "Come, then, and join this holy band, and on to glory go!"

ENDNOTES

1. Charles G. Finney, *Autobiography*, Ch. 2, 23 Jan. 2002. <http://bible.christiansunite.com/Charles_Finney/finney02.shtml>.

2. Jim W. Goll, *The Lost Art of Intercession*, (Shippensburg, PA, Revival Press, an imprint of Destiny Image Publishers, Inc., 1997) pp. 4-5.

3. Geoff Waugh, "Revival Fire," *Renewal Journal #1*, (93:1), pp. 33-65, 23 Jan. 2002. <http://www.revival-library.org/catalogues/history/waugh/05.ihtml>

4. Geoff Waugh, *Flashpoints of Revival* (Shippensburg, PA: Revival Press, an imprint of Destiny Image Publishers, Inc., 1998), pp. 56-57.

5. Waugh, *Flashpoints*, p. 57.

Chapter Nine

Revive Us Again!

Holy passion will be the very heartbeat of the coming endtime move of the Holy Spirit. It will be a passionate love for God, the love of the Bride for her Bridegroom, the love between fathers and mothers and their sons and daughters. It will be the love of the heavenly Father poured out into and through His children.

The Father longs to release a demonstration of His sons and daughters on the stage of history. More than once the Gospels record His voice booming from Heaven regarding Jesus, "This is My beloved Son, in whom I am well-pleased." He wants to bring forth His "Elijahs" and His "Elishas," His "Jehus," His "Esthers," and His "Deborahs," present them before the world arrayed in goodness and righteousness and crowned with holiness, and say, "These are My precious children, whom I love."

God is searching intensively for offspring with whom He can keep His covenant. "For the eyes of the Lord move to and fro throughout the earth that He may strongly support those whose heart is completely His" (2 Chron. 16:9a). Heart passion for God is the key that releases the fullness of His presence and power in the lives of His children.

Although God desires to bless His people and use them to bless the earth, the devil always seeks to destroy. Satan wants to bring a curse on the sons and daughters to cut them off from their heritage and godly destiny. That is why he has so savagely attacked the family, sowing seeds of discord, distrust, and moral confusion that lead to divorce, broken lives, broken relationships, and shattered hopes and dreams. His lust for destruction is what lies behind the thriving abortion industry in America, which threatens to snuff out the promise of an entire generation. In his hatred for the truth, satan has inspired laws and philosophies that deny God and muzzle the public voice of the Church, leaving millions of American youth at the mercy of the purveyors of rationalism, relativism, and humanism.

If American, European, and other societies are to be transformed, the spiritual connection between the older, middle, and younger generations must be restored. The "generation gap" that blew wide open in the 1960s spawned on the part of the young a widespread rejection of traditional values and rebellion against authority, the effects of which are still being felt an entire generation later. Bridging that gap will require all three generations working together. Each generation must be committed to passing its values, wisdom, and authority on to the next. Believers of all ages must be willing to "stand in the gap" interceding for generational reconciliation. Otherwise, this curse of rebellion and division will never be broken and even worsen as time goes on.

THE EARTH IS THE LORD'S

Unfortunately, many evangelical Christians in America today do not expect that curse to be broken.

They cannot see the "light" because they are looking at the darkness. They do not look for a great endtime revival because their theology has conditioned them to expect only that evil will increase. This fatalistic view precludes any possibility of spiritual renewal at the end of the age because, after all, "the devil controls the world, not God." Such an attitude, although it may foster a sense of urgency with regard to evangelism, also discourages believers from any serious efforts to influence and change their culture.

The thought process goes something like, "The darkness is getting so bad, and Jesus said that this is the way it would be anyway, so why bother?" This wrong thinking adds, "Because God has relegated everything to the spiritual and not to the physical, the Church should focus solely on winning souls and wait for Christ to come and rescue it from the growing storm." But we declare it's time to wage war against these prevailing strongholds of doubt and unbelief!

The problem with this fatalistic viewpoint is that it does not give sufficient merit to the omnipotence of God. It is true that as the end approaches, evil will increase; the New Testament clearly teaches this. But it is also true that as evil increases, so does righteousness. As the tide of evil rises, God pours out His grace and mercy in greater measure. God is a sovereign King; He wants His rule extended over *everything*! Not only is He the absolute ruler of an eternal spiritual Kingdom, but, despite what some Christians seem to have been taught, He also has never abdicated His throne on the earth. Psalm 24:1 says, "The earth is the Lord's, and all it contains, the world, and those who dwell in it."

If the earth is the Lord's, then that means ultimately He is in control. Every king, every president, every ruler, every station and institution of mankind is to be under the sovereign reign of God. No matter how strong, pervasive, or even invincible they appear to be, the schemes, plans, and machinery of men are as nothing in God's eyes.

> *Why are the nations in an uproar, and the peoples devising a vain thing? The kings of the earth take their stand, and the rulers take counsel together against the Lord and against His Anointed: "Let us tear their fetters apart, and cast away their cords from us!" He who sits in the heavens laughs, the Lord scoffs at them. Then He will speak to them in His anger and terrify them in His fury: "But as for Me, I have installed My King upon Zion, My holy mountain." "I will surely tell of the decree of the Lord: He said to Me, 'Thou art My Son, today I have begotten Thee. Ask of Me, and I will surely give the nations as Thine inheritance, and the very ends of the earth as Thy possession. Thou shalt break them with a rod of iron, Thou shalt shatter them like earthenware.' " Now therefore, O kings, show discernment; take warning, O judges of the earth. Worship the Lord with reverence, and rejoice with trembling. Do homage to the Son, lest He become angry, and you perish in the way, for His wrath may soon be kindled. How blessed are all who take refuge in Him!* (Psalm 2)

God is the Lord of history and, as such, can turn it whichever way He desires. When David asks, "If the foundations are destroyed, what can the righteous do?" (Ps. 11:3), the righteous answer, "We can pray and change history." Remember, history belongs to the intercessors. One of the awesome truths of Scripture is that God can and does alter human history and circumstances because of the prayers of His people.

Human history is governed by two things: the Word of God, spoken by Him and declared by His prophets, and the intercession of His prayer warriors. Every word God utters is true; every prophecy and promise will be completely and totally fulfilled. When the foundations are destroyed the righteous can cry out to the Lord, calling forth Heaven down to earth. Cry out right now, "Thy kingdom come. Thy will be done, on earth as it is in heaven" (Mt. 6:10).

BATTLING FOR THE CULTURE

A war is raging for the soul of the nations. Humanists and naturalists say there is no God and that everything that exists came about by chance. If there are no absolutes, everything in the universe is fatalistic. This is what the children and youth of America are being taught in their schools. If this is true, if the universe runs on random selection, then there is no design, no order, no pattern, and no basis for law or government or morality. If random forces rule, then there is no basis even for discovering and describing the "laws" of physics, biology, or any other scientific discipline. In a random universe *nothing* can be known with certainty.

One of the most challenging tasks for the Church in the twenty-first century is to counter this humanistic philosophy by teaching "providential history." Providential history focuses not on randomness in nature but on intelligent, creative design. God created all things. Therefore, everything from nature to law to art to politics has design and order. God's fingerprints are all over it! God is active in the lives of people whether or not they recognize Him. He has a specific design and purpose for every person and wants everyone to come to know Him.

God also has a design and purpose for America and each nation; He brought the United States into being for a divine reason. The laws of this nation were founded on the Ten Commandments, with biblical Judeo-Christian values the foundation stones and moral force upon which American society and culture were based. From these shores a free Church in a free society has launched the greatest evangelistic and missionary enterprise in the history of the world. And the best is yet to come!

Humanism and rationalism, though, are robbing America's youth of their godly heritage by blinding them to the truth of where they came from. If America's young people don't know who they are or where they came from, how can they possibly know where they are going? It becomes the blind leading the blind falling into a ditch. The children and youth of America must be taught that they are not accidents of nature but are alive by the deliberate design of a beneficent and loving Creator who has endowed them with a holy purpose. That purpose is realized in Christ, who has called and commissioned His people to "Go...and make disciples of all the nations" (Mt. 28:19a).

For many years the Church in America, particularly the evangelical wing, has tended to divide life into two separate compartments, the sacred and the secular. In the eyes of many, the secular has been regarded as beyond redemption and outside the proper purview of the Church. As a result, the Church has until recent years focused almost exclusively on the "spiritual," giving little attention to reforming the culture. This division between sacred and secular is a false dichotomy and totally foreign to the Scriptures. All of life is sacred because all of life is under the administration of God, who is the Lord of history.

The prayers of the righteous *can and do* alter history. Society and culture can be redeemed. They must! Is Jesus deserving of anything less? Doing so requires that the people of God actively engage their culture rather than separate from it. There is always a need for pastors, preachers, ministers and missionaries, but these alone are not enough. We need Holy Spirit-empowered Christian actors, authors, and artists, radical Christian philosophers, educators, and law-makers, compassionate Christian doctors, lawyers, and engineers, faithful Christian laborers, factory workers, and business executives. The way to redeem culture is to transform it from within, not condemn it from without. It's time to be salt and light in the marketplace world!

A GENTLE AWAKENING

God does not want to bring judgment upon the nations; He would much rather pour out His grace and mercy. " 'As I live!' declares the Lord God, 'I take no pleasure in the death of the wicked, but rather that the wicked turn from his way and live. Turn back, turn back from your evil ways!' " (Ezek. 33:11a) To this end He is already moving in the land. Christ is awakening His people, leading them to new dimensions of understanding and calling them to deeper levels of commitment.

For the last 20 years or so the Lord has been wooing His Church through a gentle awakening, a series of soft kisses of intimacy He has brought to the Body of Christ. Many have stepped into the "river of His presence" and entered a time of refreshing where they have been wrapped in the warm blanket of Christ's love. They have learned how to laugh again and rediscovered the truth that the joy of the Lord is their strength. This gentle awakening, much needed by the Body of Christ, has really only just begun. We have a word for you: "Get in the river and stay there!" But this is just a prelude to and preparation for a rude awakening to follow, which will then crescendo into a global great awakening, perhaps the greatest in all of history.

As a young man on a journey, in 1982 Mike Bickle, a prayer leader in the Church of America, had an encounter with God in his hotel room in Cairo, Egypt. He sensed the

Spirit of the Lord saying to him, "I am going to change the understanding and the expression of Christianity across the face of the earth in one generation." Any such subjective word should not be automatically accepted at face value; it must be tested and confirmed. Over the 20 years since, many things have occurred in the global Body of Christ that appear to confirm the word that Mike received:

1. A truly global prayer movement has arisen that is unprecedented in Church history. Consider the millions who gather in Nigeria to combat darkness by turning on the lights of violent love through powerful all-night prayer vigils.

2. Worldwide, more Christians today than ever before in history have committed themselves to regular, ongoing fasting and prayer for revival. The Bridegroom fast and the anointing of the new Nazirites are arising.

3. There has been a dramatic rise in the number of Christians around the world who fall into the Pentecostal/charismatic/third-wave segment of the Church; according to some estimates, anywhere from one-fourth to one-third of all believers worldwide.

4. The cell Church movement, virtually unknown 20 years ago, has grown astronomically, particularly in non-western nations. The world's fastest growing church, in Bogota, Colombia, with 100,000 plus members and 23,000 cells, as well as the largest church in history, in Seoul, South Korea, with over 700,000 members, are both cell churches.

5. Much is happening with regard to the Jews and the nation of Israel. In an unprecedented event, over one million Russian-speaking Jews now live in Israel, having emigrated from the Land of the

North. Today Jews are coming to Christ in greater numbers than ever before. Although still only a trickle, it is still a noticeable increase. An indigenous Messianic movement has emerged in Israel that now numbers over 40 congregations. Messianic Jewish congregations have multiplied significantly in other countries as well, the largest congregation being in the Ukraine with over 1,000 attendees.

6. During a fast in 1983, in which Jim Goll took part, a prophecy was received that in ten years God would begin something new in the earth. A parable would be played out in the Church, the story of Joseph in the dungeon with the baker and the butler (see Gen. 40). Both the baker and butler had angered the pharaoh. In the end, the baker was executed but the butler was restored to his position. In the prophecy, the baker represented the leaven of hypocrisy in the Church, while the butler represented the new wine of the Spirit. At the end of the ten years, little "butlers" would be released who would serve the new wine in the king's presence. Indeed, "new wine" was released: a prayer movement, a new sensitivity to the issues of reconciliation, identificational intercession, and confession of generational sin. The "new wine" was served at Toronto, Pensacola, Pasadena, and other places as the Lord poured out and continues to pour out His Spirit.

All of this is part of the Lord's "gentle awakening." It is the kindness of God, who is wooing and drawing a people who have forgotten His standards. Christ wants to restore a fresh holiness movement to His people. He is trying to catch their eye before sterner measures are needed.

A RUDE AWAKENING

Whenever God sets out to correct His people, He always begins with a gentle approach. If that doesn't work, He steps up the pressure and intensity. Sometimes He must get their attention with a rude awakening or a shaking. The United States is close to that point. Some contend since September 11, 2001, that we have crossed that point. The gentle awakening of recent years is crossing over into a stronger and ruder awakening. This is not necessarily a bad thing. Every action of God toward humanity is redemptive in nature, never punitive. With everything He does God seeks to draw people to Himself. Sometimes the only way to get their attention is with shocking or uncomfortable means. Even this is redemptive because it teaches men about God and His ways. "At night my soul longs for Thee, indeed, my spirit within me seeks Thee diligently; for *when the earth experiences Thy judgments the inhabitants of the world learn righteousness*" (Is. 26:9).

The prophet Amos describes God as dropping a plumb line in the midst of His people to measure their obedience.

> *Thus He showed me, and behold, the Lord was standing by a vertical wall, with a plumb line in His hand. And the Lord said to me, "What do you see, Amos?" And I said, "A plumb line." Then the Lord said, "Behold I am about to put a plumb line in the midst of My people Israel. I will spare them no longer. The high places of Isaac will be desolated and the sanctuaries of Israel laid waste. Then shall I rise up against the house of Jeroboam with the sword"* (Amos 7:7-9).

In these verses the plumb line represents God's true and unfailing Word and His absolute standard of righteousness. He was testing the "vertical wall" of the Israelites' lives and behavior to see whether or not it was "true to plumb." It was not. Israel's sins and disobedience had reached the point where judgment was needed to bring correction.

A similar situation exists in America today. As the nation crosses the threshold of a new millennium, the Lord has dropped a plumb line in her midst to discern whether or not that which has been built not only in the Church but also in governmental and societal institutions line up with His standard. This is a prelude to a rude awakening and a drastic "chiropractic adjustment" in this nation and others around the world in preparation for the global great awakening to come.

Part of this rude awakening may very well involve the Jews and the modern nation of Israel. A few years ago on Yom Kippur, the Jewish Day of Atonement, Jim Goll had a dream in which he was given an ornately carved wooden box that resembled an old music box. When he inserted a key into the lock, the lid of the box popped open to reveal the Book of Daniel inside. The Holy Spirit spoke to him and said He was going to open up understanding of Daniel's prophecies. As he waited on the Lord, the Spirit spoke to him of Daniel 3:12-13:

> *"There are certain Jews whom you have appointed over the administration of the province of Babylon, namely Shadrach, Meshach and Abed-nego. These men, O king, have disregarded you; they do not serve your gods or worship the golden image which you have set up." Then Nebuchadnezzar in rage and anger gave orders to bring Shadrach, Meshach, and Abed-nego; then these men were brought before the king.*

As Jim relates:

The interpretation I felt the Spirit giving to me about these verses was outside the normal approach to intrepreting Scripture by considering the historical context. This came to me in a dream and was in more of a revelatory and prophetic style. I believe that we are in a crossover time right now concerning the Jewish people, for whom I have a deep love. I sensed the Spirit telling me that we are entering another time historically when the rage and anger of the "Nebuchadnezzars" of our day will once again—for a short time—be released against the Jewish people. This has happened many times throughout history, the latest and worst being barely 60 years ago amid the horrors of Hitler's Third Reich. I don't like saying this and it's hard to explain, but I am convinced that we are headed toward perilous times, not just for the Jews but for all people in every nation. At the same time I am encouraged in the belief that these days of peril will present an unprecedented window of opportunity for the Body of Christ to proclaim the gospel with great power and authority.

Because this is a subjective word it must be tested and confirmed. Time will tell whether or not I have heard the Lord correctly.

A gentle awakening has come, both to the Church and to the Jewish people, but the next stage is upon us. A rude awakening is coming in the nations, in the Church, and for the sake of the Jewish people, because it is when they are fully established in their ancestral land that the Lord will give them a new heart, a heart of flesh. The old hard heart of stone and disbelief will be taken away, the blinders will be removed, and they will proclaim, "Jesus, Yeshua, You are the Messiah!" The promise of Romans 11 will be fulfilled:

For I do not want you, brethren, to be uninformed of this mystery, lest you be wise in your own estimation, that a partial hardening has happened to Israel until the fulness of the Gentiles has come in; and thus all Israel will be saved; just as it is written, "The Deliverer will come from Zion, He will remove ungodliness from Jacob. And this is My covenant with them, when I take away their sins" (Romans 11:25-27).

When this happens, it will be "life from the dead" for the world (Rom. 11:15). It will usher in a great awakening, the greatest in history, and set the stage for the return of Christ.

A GREAT AWAKENING

The seventh chapter of Daniel records a remarkable vision that the prophet received from the Lord concerning the endtimes. In his dream Daniel saw "the four winds of heaven...stirring up the great sea" (Dan. 7:2b). Four great beasts came up from the sea. The first was a lion with wings like an eagle. Its wings were plucked and it stood on two feet like a man, and a human mind was given to it. Next came a bear eating meat. The third beast looked like a leopard with four heads and four wings. Finally, there came a fourth beast, "dreadful and terrifying and extremely strong; [with] large iron teeth" (Dan. 7:7b). It also had ten horns. Even as Daniel watched, another smaller horn grew up and replaced three of the others, which were torn out by the roots. This horn "possessed eyes like the eyes of a man, and a mouth uttering great boasts" (Dan. 7:8c).

Traditionally, these four beasts are interpreted as representing four kingdoms: the Babylonian empire, the Persian empire, the Greek empire, and the Roman empire. Many Christians today, looking through a prophetic lens, see the fourth beast also as a "revived" Roman empire of the last days, with the ten horns representing its ten constituent nations. In this view, the smaller horn with a man's eyes and a boastful mouth refers to the Antichrist. Indeed, Daniel describes this horn as "waging war with the saints and overpowering them"

(Dan. 7:21b) and identifies it as a king who would "speak out against the Most High and wear down the saints of the Highest One" (Dan. 7:25a).

The point here is not to endorse any particular endtime scenario but to acknowledge a limitation common among many Bible teachers, particularly prophetic people; they get this far and then they stop looking. They develop what could be called "revelation fixation." They see this parade of terrifying beasts and pronounce that evil will continue and proliferate right up to the end. Although this is very likely true, focusing on the growth of evil can lead to a very pessimistic and skewed view of the future.

Evil is very real in the world and is growing worse all the time. Although the final chapter of history has not yet been written on the earth, God has given through His Word a peek at the closing pages. Guess what: the good guys win! It doesn't make any sense to stop reading in mid-story, to snap the book shut just after the dastardly villain has tied the damsel in distress to the railroad track and say, "That's it, she's finished!" Press on to the end to see how the hero rescues her.

By his own admission Daniel was alarmed and terrified by his vision, but he couldn't pull his eyes away. He had to keep looking to see how things turned out. Throughout this chapter he says, "I kept looking." Daniel saw the lion with eagle's wings and he "kept looking." He saw the bear eating meat and "kept looking." He saw the leopard with four heads and four wings and "kept looking." He saw the dreadful beast with ten horns and iron teeth and "kept looking." Daniel continued watching until he saw the climax, the finale to the great story unfolding before his eyes:

> *I kept looking until thrones were set up, and the Ancient*
> *of Days took His seat; His vesture was like white snow,*
> *and the hair of His head like pure wool. His throne was*
> *ablaze with flames, its wheels were a burning fire. A river*

of fire was flowing and coming out from before Him; thousands upon thousands were attending Him, and myriads upon myriads were standing before Him; the court sat, and the books were opened. Then I kept looking because of the sound of the boastful words which the horn was speaking; I kept looking until the beast was slain, and its body was destroyed and given to the burning fire. As for the rest of the beasts, their dominion was taken away, but an extension of life was granted to them for an appointed period of time. I kept looking in the night visions, and behold, with the clouds of heaven one like a Son of Man was coming, and He came up to the Ancient of Days and was presented before Him. And to Him was given dominion, glory and a kingdom, that all the peoples, nations, and men of every language might serve Him. His dominion is an everlasting dominion which will not pass away; and His kingdom is one which will not be destroyed (Daniel 7:9-14).

The gentle awakening is already here; the rude awakening looms on the horizon. Don't stop there, however, because the story is not finished yet. Beyond the rude awakening waits the greatest awakening, the prelude to the climax of the ages, the return of Christ to receive His Kingdom. Evil and calamity lie at every hand. This is only the natural deterioration of a society and a world that have gone awry, denying and turning away from God. No one on earth can yet see the complete picture. Even prophetic vision is veiled to some degree. Paul wrote, "For we know in part, and we prophesy in part; but when the perfect comes, the partial will be done away" (1 Cor. 13:9-10). Keep looking and keep praying. Don't fear the rude awakening, for beyond it lies something far greater and far grander. "See Me," says the Lord!

CATCHING THE VISION

God's Word rules over the earth and governs the affairs of men. Unlike human beings, God never speaks just to hear His own voice. Whenever God speaks—and He is speaking all the time—He speaks with purpose. Whenever God purposes to do something in the world He speaks to His people, calling them to prepare the way. "Surely the Lord God does nothing unless He reveals His secret counsel to His servants the prophets" (Amos 3:7). When God was ready to establish a nation through whom a Savior would come, He spoke to Abram and gave him a son in his old age. When God was ready to deliver that nation from slavery in Egypt, He spoke to Moses. When God was ready to call His people back from sin and idolatry, He spoke to Elijah, Isaiah, Jeremiah, and the other prophets. When God was ready to send His Son into the world, He spoke to Mary and Joseph.

Today God is moving mightily in the world, and He is calling His people to join Him in what He is doing. He is calling forth the Annas of the temple and the John the Baptists preparing the way. He is the Lord of history, and He is looking for prophets who will declare His Word and for intercessors who will birth that word through prevailing prayer and bring it into fruition. That is what truly rules the nations.

All across the land, believers young and old are rallying to His call. They are committing themselves to lives of radical abandonment to Christ—modern Nazirites who live for His holy purposes alone. They are rising up as latter-day Elijahs, Elishas, and Jehus, declaring no tolerance any longer for the Jezebelic corruption that has so thoroughly infected society. They are embracing the "Esther mandate," willing to take a stand for truth and righteousness regardless of the personal cost.

Thousands of people are dedicating themselves to prayer and fasting for revival and for the turning of America and the nations back to God. The Lord has raised up prayer and renewal movements like Promise Keepers, *The Call*, the Strategic Prayer Network, Intercessors for America, and countless others, and many are responding. None of this would be happening unless God was preparing for a major shift. He can turn the nation and the world. He wants to do it and has invited His people to join Him in it. What a responsibility, but oh what a privilege!

Many believers across the country are catching the vision that America can be changed and a great awakening ushered in. They are waking up to the necessity, even urgency, of living lives of uncompromising holiness and obedience to Christ and persistent fasting and prayer. These are the things that have always moved God. Whenever God called corporate fasts in the Old Testament, something always changed in the heavens; the same principle applies today. The call of the hour is to holiness and humility, to fasting and prayer, and to seeking God's face. At stake is the destiny of the nations. At stake is the future of the world.

> *If I shut up the heavens so that there is no rain, or if I command the locust to devour the land, or if I send pestilence among My people, and My people who are called by My name humble themselves and pray, and seek My face and turn from their wicked ways, then I will hear from heaven, will forgive their sin, and will heal their land* (2 Chronicles 7:13-14).

O Lord, revive us again!

Chapter Ten

The Call to Prayer and Fasting

s the United States teeters between mercy and judgment, it is time for the American Church to take a pulse and determine its true heart condition. Straightforward confession and heartrending repentance are in order because much of the responsibility for the nation's moral and spiritual decay lies squarely at the Church's very own doorstep. For many years evangelical and charismatic Christians virtually ignored any significant social, cultural, or civic engagement, regarding them as unimportant next to the business of saving souls. At the same time the "social gospel church" attended to the needs of the poor but often denied the authentic power of the gospel to deliver and transform lives. As a result, many nonbelievers today consider the Church to be irrelevant and woefully out of touch.

Is the Church irrelevant in modern America? Has the "salt of the earth" lost its savor? Has the "light of the world" hidden its lamp under a bushel? Are "Mary and Martha" too far apart, never to be brought together for effective service?

During recent decades the Church sat largely silent while the nation's godly heritage was gradually stripped away through legislation and court decisions. Almost without a fight the people of God yielded the field to the enemies of truth, surrendering biblical principles and values to the God-denying forces of humanism and rationalism. The enemy sowed tares in the field while the Church slept. The Church fiddled while Rome burned.

Jesus defined the proper balance between Church and state when He said, "Render to Caesar the things that are Caesar's, and to God the things that are God's" (Mk. 12:17). Much of the country's problems stem from the fact that the Church has rendered to Caesar things that never were Caesar's to start with, yielding to the state prerogatives that God never gave to the state. God never gave the state jurisdiction over public prayer or the authority to regulate personal expressions of faith. He never assigned to the state the right to define the parameters or relative value of human life, whether unborn or otherwise. God never relegated to the state the prerogative to redefine the family or to rewrite moral standards according to personal whim so that virtually anything is "acceptable." God never rendered these things to Caesar; but the Church did. We, the blood-bought Church of Jesus Christ, surrendered them through inattention and neglect.

In the early 1960s, when the school prayer issue was being decided in the courts, the general response of the Church, except for a few bold and lonely voices, was a thundering silence. After *Engle v. Vitale* became law in 1962, Lou was told that a nationally known and respected church leader said, "Now we legally can no longer pray in school. We need to be obedient."

Was he right? Consider some of the "fruit" of this obedience. Crime increased. So did teenage suicides, pregnancies, and sexually transmitted diseases. Humanistic philosophy gained control of public education. Moral behavior took a nosedive. Unanchored by traditional biblical values and faith in God, countless Americans drifted into eastern religions and New Age philosophy.

What would have happened if American Christians had risen up in the boldness of the Holy Spirit and defied *Engle v. Vitale?* How would history be different if Christian students had gathered by the thousands in school prayer meetings across the country? Like Daniel, many would have gone to a lions' den. There's a lions' den for every intercessor. But if we had, maybe our prayers for revival in our schools would have been answered like Daniel's.

Christians have a biblical responsibility to be good citizens and respect the legitimate authority of the state, as long as the state does not require them to act in a manner contrary to the laws and will of God. We are not attempting to incite an independent, rebellious spirit. The primary issue here is not even as much "civil disobedience" but "biblical obedience"!

Sometimes it is necessary for the people of God to *stand up* to the state and say, "Enough! This is wrong because it goes against the laws of God." Now is such a time in America. God has never abdicated His throne. He wants to restore in the hearts of His people a spirit of holy, humble, respectful, but firm resistance to unbiblical and "unlawful" actions of the state. In these days the Lord is calling His Church into a massive wave of prayer and fasting to change history and break the strongholds of the demonic powers of darkness over the land. The answer to America's problems is for the Body of Christ to give themselves to a long-term season of prayer and fasting, and to determine to no longer surrender to the public sector those things which are to be determined by a Higher Court and the most Supreme Judge of the universe.

CHANGING THE NATION'S ATMOSPHERE THROUGH PRAYER

Retreating from society is not the way to change history. The challenge to all believers and followers of Christ is to remain actively engaged and involved in the culture, transforming it from within. Peter, James, and John could not remain on the mountain of transfiguration with Jesus; they had to return to the valley of human need and suffering. Inspiration may come on the mountaintop, but the work is done in the valley. Mary and Martha can be joined together—and must!

Part of that work is faithful prayer for the nation, its people, and its leaders. Paul wrote to Timothy:

> *First of all, then, I urge that entreaties and prayers, petitions and thanksgivings, be made on behalf of all men, for kings and all who are in authority, in order that we may lead a tranquil and quiet life in all godliness and dignity. This is good and acceptable in the sight of God our Savior, who desires all men to be saved and to come to the knowledge of the truth* (1 Timothy 2:1-4).

Try to imagine what might happen if the American Church as a whole (or any other nation) got serious about praying for the nation's leaders instead of criticizing them so much. Such prayer could completely change the atmosphere of the country, producing a spiritual environment conducive for both preaching the gospel and responding to it. Prayer could establish a comfortable climate in which many people would "be saved and...come to the knowledge of the truth" and in which they could "lead a tranquil and quiet life in all godliness and dignity." The evil forces at work in the land care nothing for godliness or human dignity, and the last thing they want is for people to know the truth and be saved. Hey, how about this—let's go on a fast of criticism and let's do a feast of praying!

Right now the Lord has America in a crucible, and it is up to the Body of Christ to alter destiny through fasting and prayer, to turn the tide in the nation from judgment to blessing. Join in with us and the voices of others to pray to God that He would raise up godly leaders in the schools of America, teachers whose Christian influence in the classroom would prevail over the humanistic bent of modern educational philosophy. Pray for Christian legislators and jurists who will enact and enforce laws that honor God and conform to the standards of His Word. Pray for pastors and other church leaders to have the boldness to address politics, abortion, and other controversial subjects from an uncompromising and solidly biblical approach. God has never yielded political or social issues to the devil, and the Church must not either.

Even as America fights an international war against terrorism, it lies on the brink of another even greater war at home. It is a new civil war of sorts, a war for the minds and spirits of America's youth, where the sons and daughters of the newest generation could be lost by the thousands unless God moves in a massive revival and changes their hearts. Another Jesus movement is breaking out. The youth of America are going to be driven by passion, either passion for Jezebel or passion for Jesus. Let the mighty army of the Lord arise and go forth in prayer and fasting! Let the spiritual fathers and mothers intercede for God to bring forth "double portion" sons and daughters who will not succumb to the seductions of Jezebel but stand in the gap for truth, clothed in the righteousness of Christ, and ablaze with the purifying fire of holiness.

The Lord is ready to pour out His Spirit across this land and bring a violent spiritual awakening to the nation. He is jealous not only for the hearts and love of His own people but also for the hearts of those who do not yet know Him. Jesus is Lord, and He will brook no rivals. He is ready to cast down and judge the Jezebel spirit in the land and gather a spiritual harvest greater than any other in history. We believe it! Do you?

BLAZING EYES OF HOLY LOVE

J esus is jealous for His people. He will not tolerate any Jezebels that lead them astray from following Him. In days when Jezebel rules in the land, Christ reveals Himself in power and authority. Consider His words to the church in Thyatira:

> And to the angel of the church in Thyatira write: The Son of God, who has eyes like a flame of fire, and His feet are like burnished bronze, says this: "I know your deeds, and your love and faith and service and perseverance, and that your deeds of late are greater than at first. But I have this against you, that you tolerate the woman Jezebel, who calls herself a prophetess, and she teaches and leads My bond-servants astray, so that they commit acts of immorality and eat things sacrificed to idols. And I gave her time to repent; and she does not want to repent of her immorality. Behold, I will cast her upon a bed of sickness, and those who commit adultery with her into great tribulation, unless they repent of her deeds. And I will kill her children with pestilence; and all the churches will know that I am He who searches the minds and hearts; and I will give to each one of you according to your deeds. But I say to you, the rest who are in Thyatira, who do not hold this teaching, who have not known the deep things of Satan, as they call them—I place no other burden on you. Nevertheless what you have, hold fast until I come. And he who overcomes, and he who keeps My deeds until the end, to him I will give authority over the nations; and he shall rule them with a rod of iron, as the vessels of the potter are broken to pieces, as I also have received authority from My

Father; and I will give him the morning star. He who has
an ear, let him hear what the Spirit says to the churches"
(Revelation 2:18-29).

When Jezebel rises up to take over by trying to remove
every vestige of godly inheritance in the land, Jesus reveals
Himself not in the humility of a baby in a manger but in the
majesty of the King of kings and Lord of lords. He appears
not as a gentle teacher riding on a donkey but as a flaming
firebrand for His Father, cleansing the temple with a whip of
cords.

Jesus' eyes are "like a flame of fire." To His enemies it is
the fire of anger, wrath, and judgment, but to His children it
is the fire of holy love, a jealous love that will tolerate no
rivals. He says to His Church, "I have this against you, that
you tolerate the woman Jezebel...." It's not enough simply not
to commit outward acts of unfaithfulness or disobedience.
The Lord's blazing eyes pierce hearts and minds, searching
deeply for any signs of inward toleration.

The Elijah Revolution calls believers of every generation
to burn in their hearts with the holy fire of the Lord. Fathers
and mothers, sons and daughters alike, lift high the revolutionary cry, "No toleration!" The day of decision is near: awakening and revival or judgment and destruction. All are in God's
hands, but God's people can turn His hand through prayer
and fasting. Remember, history belongs to the intercessors.

NO AGE LIMIT

There was a time when the Church as a whole regarded preadolescent and teenage believers as "Christians in waiting"; followers of Jesus who nevertheless were not
"ready" to take any significant role in the work of God's Kingdom. They were not "old enough" to make any real contribu-
tion or for the Lord to use them in any meaningful way.
Thankfully, that attitude is changing in many quarters.

There is no age limit for being used by God. In fact, if you are authentically born again and filled with the Holy Spirit, you need to know that there isn't such a thing as a "baby Holy Spirit"! If you got it, you got Him! There are no "second-stringers" in the Church; every believer is called to the field. The call to follow Christ is immediately a call to war. Age is not a factor with God; neither is outward appearance. If these characteristics were important, would God ever have chosen David—the smallest and youngest in his family—to be king of Israel? Would He have chosen Esther to be queen or Mary to be the mother of His Son? Both of these women were very likely teenagers when they played their part in God's plan. God would not have chosen stammering Moses or kids like Jeremiah or Timothy. He would not have paid attention to an old widow like Anna either.

God looks at the heart. He can use any believer of any age or physical condition. All that is required is a submissive and willing spirit and a heart burning with passion for Jesus. Just say, "Here I am; use me!"

Some time ago Lou's son Jesse, who was 11 years old at the time, had a dream that illustrates this truth. In his dream Jesse saw a group of people who were fighting against gangs and violence. He wanted to be a part of that group. Jesse went to the leader of the group and asked, "How old do you have to be to join?" The leader replied, "Well, the rules have changed. Once you had to be 21, but now you only have to be 12." This dream was an invitation to the next generation to be about their Father's business at a very young age.

At the age of 12 Jesus was already about His Father's business. The rules *have* changed. Christ is saying that He wants the younger generation of His followers to rise up and be about His Father's business even at the tender age of 12. There is no need to make them wait until they are older. Let them start now! Let them pray for their friends and family and nation! Let them go on fasts for the winning of their schools! The Lord wants to release these young believers into the serious work of His Kingdom.

What would happen in the Church and across the land if thousands of young believers pledged to "tithe" their teenage years to the Lord? The seven years from age 13 to age 19, is a tithe—one-tenth—of the average life span of 70 years. What if these Christian kids committed their best to the Lord for those years, saying to Him, "I will be wholly abandoned to You!" God would use them in ways far beyond anything they could possibly imagine. At the end of that time, they would discover that they never again want to live any other way. If we are going to be radical, well, let's do it!

An Upper Room Network

In First Kings 17:17-24 (just before his dramatic confrontation on Mount Carmel with the prophets of Baal), Elijah restored to life the son of a poor widow. The prophet took the boy to the upper room where he was living, placed him on the bed, and stretched himself out three times over the child's body. He prayed, "O Lord my God, I pray Thee, let this child's life return to him" (1 Kings 17:21b). God heard Elijah's prayer and answered him; the boy came back to life.

A similar experience occurred in the life of Elisha, Elijah's next-generation spiritual son. Once again a woman's young son had died. The woman had been very kind to Elisha, and God had blessed her with a son. Now the child was dead. When Elisha entered the boy's room, where he was lying on the bed, he closed the door and prayed to God. "And he went up and lay on the child, and put his mouth on his mouth and his eyes on his eyes and his hands on his hands, and he stretched himself on him; and the flesh of the child became warm. Then he returned and walked in the house once back and forth, and went up and stretched himself on him; and the lad sneezed seven times and the lad opened his eyes" (2 Kings 4:34-35).

Part of the heart of the Elijah Revolution is for believers to take "dead" children and teenagers to the "upper room" and stretch themselves out over them in prayer. Such an "upper room" network must come to be in America if there is any hope of saving our young people. Hell has released such a rage of hatred and destruction on this young generation that "normal" prayer will not work. Believers must move beyond their normal ways and stretch themselves out in fasting and prayer for the salvation of this generation, to raise them from the dead, so to speak. In fact, let's believe for a big miracle. How about the Church being raised from the dead?!

What would happen if "upper room" networks began to form in every city, in every church, and on every school campus across America, where parents and children alike gathered to fast and pray to raise young people from the dead and to bring awakening to the nation? What would happen if three generations united in a continuous season of fasting and prayer for the turning and salvation of America? That is why we have included a 21-Day Prayer Guide at the close of this book. These prayers, promises, and devotions are written by young radical believers for us all to join together and lift up to the Lord who answers prayer. Join us. Unite with us. Let *The Call* go forth!

It Can Happen Again

It has happened before. The Great Awakening of the 1730s and 1740s provided the moral and spiritual fiber that lay behind the establishment of the United States on biblical and godly principles and values. In 1859 a great prayer revival swept many of the largest cities in America, which many historians credit with providing the spiritual foundation that enabled the country to survive four years of civil war.

Every awakening and revival has been preceded by a season of prayer and fasting. It is a bedrock spiritual principle that prayer and fasting shifts things in the heavens and changes the destiny of nations on earth. The power lies not in the fasting and praying, but in a God who responds to the fasting and prayers of His people. Remember what the Lord spoke to Jim in Czech Republic on his journey to redig the Moravian Watch of the Lord? "Have you ever considered the multi-dimensional direction of prayer? Remember, what goes up, must come down!"[1]

The call has gone out! A great revolution is underway! The Lord is raising up a new generation of radical revolutionaries: Elijahs, Elishas, Jehus, Esthers, Deborahs, and Nazirites who are fired with passion for Jesus and are committed to live fully and completely for Him alone, whatever the cost. Their lives are marked by holiness and a steadfast refusal to compromise with the Jezebel spirit in the land. They are stretching themselves out as living sacrifices, offering themselves up in fasting and prayer for the turning of a nation and the salvation of its people. They are the Bride making ready for her Bridegroom, and their hearts echo with the cry, "Come, Lord Jesus!"

It is time for the Church to rise up and take a stand!

Rise up, O [church] of God!
Have done with lesser things;
Give heart and mind and soul and strength
To serve the King of kings.
Rise up, O [church] of God!
His kingdom tarries long;
Bring in the day of brotherhood
And end the night of wrong.[2]

The call for passion and sacrifice for radical change is being issued. Will you say, "Yes, Lord," to this Elijah Revolution and sign on the dotted line?

_____   _____
Name   Date

ENDNOTES

1. Jim W. Goll, *The Lost Art of Intercession*, (Shippensburg, PA, Revival Press, an imprint of Destiny Image Publishers, Inc., 1997) p. 78.

2. William P. Merrill, "Rise Up, O Men of God," public domain.

Appendix

Radical Prayers for Elijah's Revolution

The following is a 21-day prayer guide written by young people to help target our intercession. The writings of each day's devotion include a **Scripture Promise**, a **Devotional Reflection**, and a closing **Intercessory Prayer**. This guide can be used as a prayer guide for any of The Call events, citywide outreaches, for churches, youth groups, or your own life personally. Just take advantage of this radical prayer guide and do it!

DAY 1

Scripture Promise

Are not two sparrows sold for a penny? Yet not one of them will fall to the ground apart from the will of your Father. And even the very hairs of your head are all numbered. So don't be afraid; you are worth more than many sparrows (Matthew 10:29-31 NIV).

...A voice of one calling in the desert, "Prepare the way for the Lord, make straight paths for him" (Luke 3:4 NIV).

Devotional Reflection

Throughout the ages, history has been written by ordinary men dreaming for the extraordinary to occur. Today God has again extended that call and has opened up a window of opportunity for young and old alike to pen the future of this great nation. In light of the recent attacks on America, there is a generation not marked by age that is arising from the ashes to reclaim the Divine destiny of this nation. Just as Benjamin Franklin proclaimed over 200 years ago, "*God governs in the affairs of men.* And if a sparrow cannot fall to the ground without his notice, *is it possible that an empire can rise without his aid?*" The only hope for America is in God, but God has handed us a letter of invitation, through Joel 2 to change the course of this nation. We must arise and become a voice crying out in the wilderness to turn this nation back to Him. God is looking today for sold-out radical revolutionaries to be a "voice" and not just a mere echo in this kairos period. Voices must arise who will not only cry out to God, but also to this nation to overturn the ungodly atheistic and secularist decrees of *Engle v. Vitale* and *Roe v. Wade.* The battle cannot be lost. We need to believe. If God can do it once, He can do it again.

Intercessory Prayer

"God, do it again in our land. Father, raise up a generation of sold-out radical 'voices' who will rock this nation back to You. We respond to the call that has gone forth and ask You to arise and shine through the darkness. We cry out to You in desperation, asking that You would raise up men and women like Daniel of old. God, if You can do it once, surely You can do it again."

–Brian

Day 2

Scripture Promise

One thing have I desired of the Lord, that will I seek after; that I may dwell in the house of the Lord all the days of my life, to behold the beauty of the Lord... (Psalm 27:4 KJV).

Devotional Reflection

This word *behold* means to have a fixed gaze. As we behold His holiness, His beauty captivates us and the beauty of this world begins to fade. Something far greater captures our affections. As we behold His beauty, we are drawn ever nearer and nearer to Him. His holiness does not drive us away in shame; it fascinates our hearts and transcends our minds so that our only response is to get closer to this beauty. It is as we behold the beauty of His holiness that our appetite for His presence is increased and our former appetites for the things of this world wane. It is through this captivated heart we are made holy, as we are fascinated by His holiness and ever seek to move closer to this beauty. We are not made holy by our works or sacrifice, but as the very longings of our heart are captivated and all we truly long for is Him.

Intercessory Prayer

"Lord, fascinate my heart with the beauty of Your holiness. Let my heart behold true beauty. I long that my gaze would be fixed upon You; I consecrate my eyes to You; fill them with longing for You. Let my life be marked by a passion to see You. I will spend my life seeking You alone. There is none that compares to You."

–Bethany

DAY 3

Scripture Promise

> *...and Elijah passed by* [Elisha], *and cast his mantle upon him. And he left the oxen, and ran after Elijah...and took a yoke of oxen, and slew them, and boiled their flesh with the instruments of the oxen...Then he arose, and went after Elijah, and ministered unto him* (1 Kings 19:19-21 KJV).

Devotional Reflection

God is calling young Elishas to give one year of their lives to fasting and prayer. Has a spiritual father cast his mantle over you? Run with him; fast, pray, and travel together. History's mantles are falling: Frank Bartleman travailed for one year, and he burned and birthed the Azusa Street revival. One year, and the returns are geometric; ten years of avoided mistakes and the launching of a friendship with God.

Intercessory Prayer

"God, I feel Your burning call. I say 'yes!' I ask for the anointing to fast and pray in Jesus' name. God, give me the mantles of my fathers, of Bartleman and Elijah. I give myself over to a season where my heart can burn unbridled. Give me a year full of encounters with You, a whirlwind year that will rock me forever in Jesus' name."

–Abbott

DAY 4

Scripture Promise

Read Daniel chapters 6 and 10.

Devotional Reflection

Thousands of years ago, the king of Babylon, Darius, issued a decree that no man could pray, except to him, for 30 days. Anyone who committed this "crime" would be put to death. Even still, Daniel, a prophet of old who had been *forged in the womb of the prayer closet,* chose to obey the laws of God rather than those of man. He had developed the daily custom of coming before the throne of the true King thrice daily and refused to allow anyone to tell him otherwise. Daniel knew that true authority and power belonged to the Throne above and he refused, even in the face of the lion's mouth, to forsake the one and true King. King Darius could not understand Daniel's decision. The decree was issued for only 30 days...could Daniel not give up his prayer life for just 30 days? *Absolutely not!* Daniel refused to set aside the transcending love of coming before the Father, no matter the cost. Eventually, Daniel's consistent prayer life resulted in freedom from slavery for his people and a visitation from Heaven. WOW!

Daniel understood that there was contention in the heavens over God's people. It took 21 days of fervent and effective prayer before breakthrough would occur in his life and the breakthrough for his nation. However, he had been the contender for his people for many years before that kairos moment, and it was the quality of his life that made him highly esteemed.

So it was in Daniel's day thousands of years ago, and so it is today. The gods of this age shut the Church out of the daily life of America, but godliness will again prevail. Just as God had strategically placed Daniel in Babylon, so God is again developing a generation of prophets to issue an eviction notice to the principalities and strongholds that have overstayed their welcome. But remember, prophets are forged in the womb of the prayer closet, and prayer is caught, not taught. You are highly esteemed!

Intercessory Prayer

"God, we join with the prayers that Daniel prayed over his nation thousands of years ago, and we ask that You would turn nations back to You. Rather, we stand to contend on behalf of this nation and our world. God, make us contenders in this day and age."

–Brian

DAY 5

Scripture Promise

Jesus, full of the Holy Spirit, returned from the Jordan and was led by the Spirit in the desert, where for forty days He was tempted by the devil. He ate nothing during those days, and at the end of them He was hungry (Luke 4:1-2 NIV).

Jesus returned to Galilee in the **power** *of the Spirit, and news about Him spread through the whole countryside* (Luke 4:14 NIV).

Devotional Reflection

Jesus and John the Baptist had their days in the wilderness, their places of separation to God. It is in the wilderness that John was refined and prepared to influence his world. (Oh, how God wants you to influence your world for Him!) It is in the wilderness where Jesus added power to the in-filling of the Holy Spirit. Pure and simple, the wilderness is a place of preparation.

Today, if you dare, you can be refined. Today, if you dare, you can be prepared for the Master's use. Today, if you dare, you can add power to your in-filling of the Holy Spirit. How can that be? How do I find my wilderness? By the mercy and grace of God there is a heaven-sent, self-imposed wilderness: the *fast.* Yes, it is a place of refining, a place of preparation, and a place of power. Preparation for what, you might ask? For more than you think.

Get extreme today. Separate yourself from the things you deserve! So you've been good—that's great. Be better than good—be cleansed and used by God!

Intercessory Prayer

"God, I want to be refined. I ask You to remove the dross of compromise from my life. Burn up the dead wood of self-centeredness in my life. I want to bear abundant fruit for You. Prepare me for what lies ahead, even that which I won't understand at the time. Add power to my life that I might represent You well! I want to serve the purpose of God in my generation."

–Kristina

DAY 6

Scripture Promise

I tell you the truth: Among those born of women there has not risen anyone greater than John the Baptist; yet he who is least in the kingdom of heaven is greater than he (Matthew 11:11 NIV).

Devotional Reflection

You are destined for greatness. When Jesus made this statement, He was ushering in a new age. Up until that time there was no one greater than John the Baptist. According to Jesus, John was one of the greatest men born of a woman.

Under the law, the life of John the Baptist could not be exceeded. But, with the born-again experience, it can. Even the least of those who are born of God are greater than John the Baptist. That means you and me. John the Baptist was "more than a prophet" and the "Elijah to come," yet his life will be surpassed by us, the nameless and faceless who are birthed by the Spirit of God.

Intercessory Prayer

"God, thank You for giving me greatness through the blood of Your Son. May my life reflect the greatness You have bestowed upon me."

–Cheryl

Day 7

Scripture Promise

Who may ascend the hill of the Lord? Who may stand in His holy place? He who has clean hands and a pure heart... (Psalm 24:3-4a NIV).

Devotional Reflection

We are on the verge of seeing widespread demonstrations of God's miraculous power all over America. The blind will see, the deaf will hear, the lame will walk, the dead will be raised, and people will be healed of cancer and AIDS. I have no doubt that God is getting ready to move in this way once again. The question is, will God's people consecrate themselves for such a move, and will our integrity be intact?

Just because a person is powerfully anointed to do any of the miracles mentioned above, does not mean that he or she is walking holy before the Lord. In revival history, sometimes God has chosen people living in sin to be conduits of His healing power. But that does not mean this is what He desires. Before Joshua and the Israelites crossed the Jordan, he commanded them to consecrate themselves (see Josh. 3:5). God is saying the same thing to us today!

It is time to become a person of strong character living in the light of God's holiness! It is time to throw off our habits of besetting sin and iniquity! It is time for us to believe that God's grace "teaches us to say 'No' to ungodliness and worldly passions, and to live self-controlled, upright and godly lives in this present age" (Tit. 2:12).

Intercessory Prayer

"Heavenly Father, I ask that You would make me a person of integrity. I pray that You would enrapture me with Your love and loose me from the chains of sin and compromise in my life. Thank You for saving me and forgiving *all* of my sins!"

–Billy

Day 8

Scripture Promise

"Return, O backsliding children," says the Lord; *"for I am married to you..."* (Jeremiah 3:14 NKJV).

Devotional Reflection

We are at a time in history like Jeremiah of old, the weeping prophet who stood calling the nation of Israel to return to Him for they had forsaken Him. Much like Israel, we have become the unfaithful wife of Jehovah. Over and over throughout the Old Testament we hear the prophets crying out on behalf of God to His people: "You have forgotten Me and chased after other lovers; you have played the harlot, yet return to Me, return to Me, for I am married to you."

The very essence of marriage is that we give ourselves completely to one and guard ourselves from all others. When we see the word *lovers,* it refers to having affection for (sexually or otherwise). Our affections is what we exercise our mind toward, what we give our thoughts to and our attention to, what the passion of our heart is for, what our desire is toward, what we yield our feelings or sensitive nature to. It is the warm feeling in the midriff of the body. This is what the Lord is jealous for—that our very affections would be reserved for Him.

The word *harlot* refers to idolatry. Because Israel was regarded as the wife of Jehovah, to commit idolatry was to commit spiritual adultery. It is the jealousy of God that burns for a faithful bride that will not serve Him out of obligation or religious duty...a bride that is not only legally married but truly joined...a bride that has forsaken all other loves and consecrated her heart unto one.

Intercessory Prayer

"Lord, I consecrate my affections to You, that I would not burn with the lust of the flesh but with the fire of Your jealousy. Possess my heart and make it Your own. I place You as the seal upon my heart that I would be ravished by You. Let my very affections burn for You."

–Bethany

DAY 9

Scripture Promise

Behold, you are fair, my love! Behold, you are fair! (Song of Solomon 4:1 NKJV)

Devotional Reflection

The Shulamite developed a heart of devotion by listening, gazing upon, and receiving the King's devotion to her. Devotion does not come by simply trying harder or making yourself more committed. Devotion comes when the Great I Am tells you who you are and what you look like to Him.

In chapters 2 and 3, the Shulamite had been disobedient to the King's call. He goes away, and then she tries to find Him. When she finally finds Him, the first words out of His mouth were, "You are fair, my love." What a surprise! The Shulamite must have been thinking, *I just blew it big time, and He's calling me beautiful. He must really love me.* Countless times He shows her sweet acts of devotion and tenderly tells her the beauty He sees in her. This causes her heart to swell with devotion.

Intercessory Prayer

"Great I Am, tell me who I am to You. Desire of the Nations, cause my eyes to see Your devotion to me. Cause my ears to hear what You think about me, and cause my heart to feel how You feel toward me."

–Cheryl

DAY 10

Scripture Promise

See, I will send you the prophet Elijah before that great and dreadful day of the Lord comes. He will turn the hearts of the fathers to their children, and the hearts of the children to their fathers; or else I will come and strike the land with a curse (Malachi 4:5-6 NIV).

Devotional Reflection

There is a shift taking place in this hour. It is the hearts of fathers turning to their children and the hearts of children turning to their fathers. All of creation is groaning for this hour. What happens in God's heart when the generations come together? When they join their hearts in unison with prayer? How powerful is prayer? How much greater it is when a father joins with his son to pray, or a mother joins with a daughter to pray. In the Gospel of John, chapter 17, you can almost feel the joy and pleasure of the Father as He and His Son Jesus communed in prayer. The eternal heart of God that beats for the generations is so pleased when two or three generations come together and approach His throne! But, there is an enemy that wants to keep you separated from your parents. It allows him to bring a curse on the land.

Young man, young woman, go find your parents right now. Parents, go find your sons and daughters. Ask them to come and pray with you—to pray and ask God's favor and blessing on your family and on your neighbors. If your children are not living at home, call them. They want to hear from you. Ask them to pray on the phone with you. (Maybe there are hurts or reasons you shouldn't pray together. Don't let that stop you; imitate Jesus and lay down your hurts and your need to be right.)

Intercessory Prayer

"Lord, I ask You to bless my mom and dad. I ask You to restore our relationship wherever it is needed. Give me grace to receive them as a blessing in my life.

"Lord, I ask You to bless my son or daughter. I ask You to forgive me when I have hurt them. Forgive me, Father, when I have put my needs above theirs.

"Today we ask Your blessing on our family. Help us to love each other, honor each other, and serve each other."

–Kristina

DAY 11

Scripture Promise

It is not good to have zeal without knowledge, nor to be hasty and miss the way (Proverbs 19:2 NIV).

Devotional Reflection

I believe that this verse can be used to describe the importance of the generations joining together to see God's purposes accomplished. The young generation that God is raising up right now is full of unabated passion for Him and zeal for His glory to be known. The generation that has gone before them is full of knowledge and wisdom from their numerous experiences with God that young people do not have. There must be a marriage of the generations so that "zeal" and "knowledge" will flow together and rub off on each other.

In the late 1960s and early 70s God sparked a revival known as the "Jesus Movement." Radical young people were performing miracles and thousands were getting saved! Yet, the movement quickly died and was aborted before it reached its full potential. This is because the church "fathers" refused to embrace the movement due to some of its excesses, and the "sons" felt misunderstood and did not want to receive any correction that would have been beneficial to them.

I would encourage every person who is reading this to ask God for a spiritual father or mother. Likewise, every adult should be looking to impart his or her life into a spiritual son or daughter. Let us learn from our past mistakes, look beyond our generational differences, and run hard after the God of Abraham, Isaac, and Jacob!

Intercessory Prayer

"Heavenly Father, I ask that You would join the young and the old in the next move of Your Spirit. I pray that a deep bonding and love would exist between the generations. Let us run together in order to see Your will accomplished!"

–Billy

DAY 12

Scripture Promise

... *"The voice of one crying in the wilderness: Prepare the way of the Lord; make His paths straight"* (Luke 3:4 NKJV).

Devotional Reflection

John the Baptist was born in a time when two worlds were on the verge of colliding. History was desperately searching for someone to connect it to the future. Four hundred years of stifling silence had given history little identity and the future little hope. John the Baptist became a voice that pulled these two worlds together through his cry.

It is this very mantle that has fallen upon a rising generation. History is calling again, desperately searching for someone to reconcile it to the future. Here we stand, a generation suspended somewhere between what has been and what is coming. Here we stand with a call to become the bridge between history and the future. Let us rise as a voice in this hour to prepare the way of the Lord.

Intercessory Prayer

"God, make me a voice that will bridge history to the future once more. I was born for such a time as this. Cause me to be someone who will prepare the way for You."

–Kristina

DAY 13

Scripture Promise

... *Your hair is like royal tapestry; the king is held captive by its tresses* (Song of Solomon 7:5 NIV).

Devotional Reflection

This verse makes it obvious that the Shulamite is a Nazarite! It is not her conquests (arms), her prophetic proclamations (mouth), or even her ministry (feet) that has taken the King captive. It is her inner devotional life to Him symbolized by her hair. The King, who took captivity captive, is taken captive by our hearts' devotion to Him. Jesus was always drawn to the town of Bethany. What was the magnet drawing Him, taking Him captive? It was the home of a woman who had chosen devotion over duty and had taken the King of kings captive by her choice.

God wants you to be a history maker as well as a captivator of His heart. Become a magnet that draws the King and have a radical devotional life of love. This devotion will never be taken from you.

Intercessory Prayer

"God, give me a heart of devotion. I want a heart that burns with never-ending passion for You. Let me become Your magnet that draws You."

–Cheryl

DAY 14

Scripture Promise

...So one of the servants of the king of Israel answered and said, "Elisha the son of Shaphat is here, who poured water on the hands of Elijah" (2 Kings 3:11 NKJV).

Devotional Reflection

Elisha served his prophet. Service, done in love and faith, is invested with spiritual power. "For even the Son of Man did not come to be served, but to serve, and to give His life a ransom for many" (Mk. 10:45). It is seed sown into the best soil: a spiritual father. Who is your prophet? Wash his hands. In other words, give rides, help with his house, anticipate his needs. Be his chief intercessor; mobilize prayer meetings. E.M. Bounds said, "The preacher must pray, and the preacher must be prayed for." Gehazi, Elisha's servant, had selfish motives: his own ministry and money. Elisha, though, when ministering to Elijah, got a passion to serve, wept for his father, and got the double portion.

Intercessory Prayer

"Lord, I pray that You link me to a prophet, a mentor. Give me the heart of Jesus to give myself in service. Set me in orbit around Your purpose. I ask not for a quick ministry, but for a dad/mom to love and serve, and a double portion inheritance."

–Abbott

DAY 15

Scripture Promise

Let no one despise your youth, but be an example to believers in word, in conduct, in love, in spirit, in faith, in purity (1 Timothy 4:12 NKJV).

Devotional Reflection

We are never too young to be examples. No matter our age, there will always be someone younger than us looking for someone older to follow. What a powerful statement Paul made to Timothy: "Let no one despise your youth, but be an example." We have a mandate to lead. There is no greater accomplishment we could have than that of leading the way through our example to those following after us. We don't have to wait until we are natural parents or old enough to be parents. We can start now. We can turn and reach behind us and pull a young generation up alongside of us. We can be examples to them in all that we say, in all that we do, and in all that we believe. Let us start now to prepare the way for those who will be following after us.

Intercessory Prayer

"God, I am never too young to follow You and to lead the way for others. I want to give my life to being an example for those coming after me. I will reach back to those younger than me and pull them alongside of me so that they too may have someone to follow. I pray that You would show me how to be more of an example in all that I do and that I would never let my age keep me from being totally devoted to You."

–Kristina

DAY 16

Scripture Promise

While I am in the world, I am the light of the world (John 9:5 NIV).

Devotional Reflection

When I was growing up, I remember my pastor saying, "If God calls you to be a missionary, don't settle to become president of the United States!" That statement is 100 percent true, but the reverse of it is also true. If God calls you to become president of the United States, don't settle for becoming a missionary!

We as Christians must understand that God calls us to influence and redeem every arena of culture. The highest calling for a Christian is not to become a pastor or missionary. Our highest calling is to love God with all of our hearts and serve our fellow man in whatever occupation He has called us to. There are young Nazirites out there who are called of God to be the next movie stars, musicians, artists, news reporters, business executives, and political leaders. We are called to redeem the "gates of authority" in our culture, not point the finger and run away from them! It is time we take responsibility for abdicating the authority God has given us in these arenas! It is time to be a light in this world for His glory!

Intercessory Prayer

"Heavenly Father, I pray that You would raise up godly leaders in places of cultural influence. May the Church learn how to enter into the darkest places of society and be a burning and shining light for Your glory!"

–Billy

DAY 17

Scripture Promise

See, I will send you the prophet Elijah before that great and dreadful day of the Lord comes. He will turn the hearts of the fathers to their children, and the hearts of the children to their fathers; or else I will come and strike the land with a curse (Malachi 4:5-6 NIV).

Devotional Reflection

"...that the father would *live for the dreams* of his children and that his children would *dream* to *live* for the father." –Lou Engle

William Tennent, Sr., the catalyst of the First Great Awakening, embodied the true spirit of Elijah that would turn the hearts of the father back to the children and the hearts of the children to the father. God had given thunder in the voice of William Tennent, Sr., as well as the gift of powerful preaching, but William Tennent, Sr.'s true legacy remained in his four sons. His dream was not to be known as a powerful revivalist, but to train his sons up in the way of the Lord who would, in turn, alter the very course of this nation. He created a school, derisively called by others the Log College

Seminary, for his sons in order to train them up to be history makers. And that they were.

Gilbert Tennent began to rock America with his prophetic call to awaken the slumbering Church, God's Sleeping Beauty. Gilbert had no concern for what man thought of him, but only for what the Father had called him to do. The great revivalist, George Whitefield, wrote concerning Gilbert Tennent that "Hypocrites must soon be converted or enraged at his preaching. He is a son of thunder and does not regard the face of man. He is deeply sensible of the deadness and formality of the Christian church in these parts, and has given noble testimonies against it."

Today the Church must again see sons and daughters of thunder strike again. They must shake America back to its core with their holy and passionate roars. Will God find in you a son of thunder? Will God find in America a new breed of Nazirites who know nothing but to do the will of the Father?

Intercessory Prayer

"Father, we thank You that even in those days, You were turning the hearts of the fathers to the children and the hearts of the children to their fathers. But, Father, we pray that this would not be the end result of the Elijah Revolution, but that it would, in turn, like it did in Gilbert Tennent, raise up sons and daughters of thunder. God, we don't want just picnic Christianity; we want a biblical, violent Christianity in the heavens and love and grace on earth!" (See Matthew 11.)

–Brian

Day 18

Scripture Promise

Then He returned to His disciples and found them sleeping. "Could you men not keep watch with Me for one hour?"... (Matthew 26:40 NIV).

Devotional Reflection

"History belongs to the intercessors who believe the future into being." –Walter Wink

In the 1850s, God began to move on the hearts of men and women all over America again just before the outbreak of the American Civil War. God laid it on the heart of Jeremiah Lamphier, a no-name businessman in New York City to reach the unchurched masses of the city. Lamphier, who had never handled anything like this before, organized a noonday prayer meeting. He printed pamphlets urging people to attend the prayer meeting and began handing them out to anyone who would take them On the day of the first prayer meeting, Lamphier waited, but no one showed up. He began to pray. Twenty minutes later, he heard the footsteps of a man trudging up the stairs. The prayer meeting had begun.

Months later, storekeepers and business owners began to close their shops at 11:55 a.m. so that their workers could rush off to the noonday prayer meetings that began with one man's simple prayer. They had one focus: to see God break out all over America. Their motivation? Jesus said, "Could you men not keep watch with Me for one hour?" Their response? Thousands around the country began to do just that! Newspapers began to report this move of God, and people all over America caught the fire and passion of their prayers. Within two years, more than one million souls had been swept into the Kingdom as a direct result of these noonday fiery, radical prayer meetings.

We need to see it happen again. Where are the radical, extreme, revolutionary men and women who will take up this call again?

Intercessory Prayer

"God, we pray that a new laymen's prayer movement would appear all over America again. Bring prayer to the vanguard of America's schoolchildren again. Put it on their hearts to seek Your face and to overturn the ungodly decree of *Engle v. Vitale*. God, it must happen. Lord, we pray that You would not find us in a deep sleep, but that we would be the ones to keep watch with You."

–Brian

DAY 19

Scripture Promise

> *...While they were still some distance from Ephrath, Rachel began to give birth and had great difficulty. And as she was having great difficulty in childbirth, the midwife said to her, "Don't be afraid, for you have another son." As she breathed her last—for she was dying—she named her son Ben-Oni. But his father named him Benjamin* (Genesis 35:16-18 NIV).

Devotional Reflection

In this passage, Rachel could represent a dying world system. Realizing that she is dying and has nothing to offer, she names her child Ben-Oni, "son of my sorrow." What a terrible beginning for a child, to be known as the one who brought sorrow, as the one responsible for the pain.

What name did society put on you? Were you labeled by those who felt they were losing the game of life and dying? By those who had to focus their pain somewhere other than on themselves? What name did your parents, your friends, or your peers put on you? Loser, stupid, ugly, less than, geek? What name have you been living under? If your father never blessed you, you are probably looking to prove yourself, but it is never enough.

Into this sorrow steps the heart of a true father. He will not let his son be marked for life as the cause of sorrow. He stands over his son and speaks destiny and future into this young life. "He will not be known as Ben-Oni, but Benjamin, 'son of my right hand'!" He is no loser; he is my son! The word *Ben* means "builder of the family name." Benjamin has a starting point, a launching place. He is connected with the past and has a future. He is to build the family name.

There is a Father wiser and more loving than even Benjamin's father. He is our Father God. He wants to give you a new name—a name that speaks of hope, a name with a future. He calls you His son and He wants you to build the family name. Let Him remove the labels, the curses, that society has placed upon you. Let Him speak to you of your future. He says He has a hope and a future, an expected end for you that is good! (See Jeremiah 29:11.)

Intercessory Prayer

"Lord, I need You. Sometimes I don't even understand how the words that were spoken over me in the past still affect me today. Speak to me, speak over my life. I want to help build Your family name, Lord. Remove the power of the wrong words that were placed upon me. I forgive those who said these things to me. Your Word says You love me. Your Word says that I am Your son! I receive You as my heavenly Father; heal any 'father wounds' in my heart. And, Lord, bring spiritual fathers into my life—men who will help me to see myself as You see me, men who will help me build the family name."

–Kristina

DAY 20

Scripture Promise

> Then [Jacob] *dreamed, and behold, a ladder was set up on the earth, and its top reached to heaven; and there the angels of God were ascending and descending on it. And*

behold, the Lord stood above it and said: "I am the Lord
God of Abraham your father... (Genesis 28:12-13
NKJV).

Devotional Reflection

God is the Eternal Dreamer. He speaks in dreams,
rustlings in the night. If we explore the dream, inquiring
about the interpretation and praying, windows from Heaven
sweep open and we're brought into His counsels. If we
believe the dream and persevere in the land of our promise,
we become His dream, issued forth from the mind of the
Father since before time, sons of Abraham who hear the
Voice, "Look at the stars, so shall your seed be."

Intercessory Prayer

"God of Abraham, Isaac, and Jacob, I worship You in
awe. Your ways are like the wind. I ask for the promise of Pen-
tecost; download dreams and visions, in Jesus' name. I
embrace the supernatural, fully expecting the Voice of God.
Speak to me in the night; throw open the windows of my destiny in Christ, in Jesus' name."

–Abbott

DAY 21

Scripture Promise

From the days of John the Baptist until now, the kingdom
of heaven has been forcefully advancing, and forceful men
lay hold of it (Matthew 11:12 NIV).

Devotional Reflection

There is an unprecedented assault upon America's
young people today. With the destruction of core family values, perversion and immorality have been unleashed against
our youth. Yet, there is still hope for America.

Elijah was a man who arrived onto the scene in Israel when the Israelites' spirituality was at an all-time low and where perversions and immorality had taken siege of the land. Striding in, seemingly out of nowhere, the prophet Elijah called the people of his nation back to the true and living God. In a showdown between this prophet and the prophets of Baal, Elijah knew that the victory was his and shouted, "How long will you waver between two opinions? If the Lord is God, follow Him; but if Baal is God, follow him" (1 Kings 18:21 NIV).

That same question is still ringing loud and clear in our day: How long will we waver between two opinions? The ruler of Elijah's day, Jezebel, had continued to defy the laws of God and had caused Israel to turn away from their destiny. Elijah came to challenge and contend for that authority over their land, and that he did. The spirit of Elijah was not merely a spirit that would turn the hearts of the fathers to the children and the children to their fathers; it also was a stance of violence and contention. We must contend in our land against principles and ideologies that have dominated for too long. Even as Jehu had commanded millenniums before to throw Jezebel down, the rumblings of a liberation army can be heard in the distance, chanting, "Throw her down! Throw her down! Throw her down!"

Intercessory Prayer

"Father, we pray for this Elijah Revolution to arise in our day. Make us contenders who will challenge the status quo of our day and not be satisfied to remain silent. Give us the faith that Elijah had to see the wickedness and immorality thrown down in his land. Father, we won't tolerate Jezebel in our land anymore; moreover, we won't tolerate her in our own hearts!"

–Brian

The Values of the Call

The Call is a movement emphasizing prayer, worship and fasting for Spiritual breakthrough. It is a nameless and faceless people movement joining the generations. Therefore, it will not be marketed as a convention of celebrities. The primary participants are young people. The musicians on stage are to be worshippers, not entertainers. The board of directors will not receive financial compensation, and speakers and leaders come at their own expense.

People should prayerfully consider fasting on the day of *The Call* event is in their city, region, or nation; no food will be provided. *The Call* is a grassroots movement. It is a cross-cultural and cross-denominational event. *The Call* espouses these definitive values: worship, unity, prayer, fasting, follow-up, transformation, repentance, reconciliation, impartation, equipping, revival, and a holy revolution.

INVOLVEMENT

You can be involved in the following ways: prayer, volunteering, providing financial support, getting the Word out, and/or becoming a revolutionary for Jesus.

FINANCIAL SUPPORT

The Call is financed primarily through individual donations. Many of *The Call* events will require no registration, but a few will require registration due to the facilities involved.

FOR MORE INFORMATION

Check out our website at: www.thecallrevolution.com

TO FINANCIALLY SUPPORT *THE CALL*

Send donations to: The Call
                            1539 E. Howard Street
                            Pasadena, CA 91104

More Equipping Tools
by Jim and Michal Ann Goll

Jim and Michal Ann Goll are the cofounders of **Ministry to the Nations**—a prophetic, intercessory and missions agency equipping believers to fulfill their call in Christ Jesus. They have launched the **Heart of David Ministry Institute**—a correspondence school—and are in the beginning phases of starting **The House of David**—a worship and prayer center. They are the parents of four wonderful children and live in the beautiful hills of Franklin, Tennessee.

The Golls are the authors of the following books: *Fire on the Altar, The Lost Art of Intercession, Encounters With a Supernatural God, Kneeling on the Promises, Women on the Frontlines, Father Forgive Us!, Wasted On Jesus, Exodus Cry,* and *The Coming Prophetic Revolution,* plus the newly released *Elijah's Revolution.*

Other Resources Include:

- *Prayers For Israel* (CD and Cassette), *Invitation to Intimacy* (CD), *Restoring David's Tabernacle* (worship CD), *The Lost Art of Intercession* (audio book both in CD and cassette), and *The Healing Presence* (CD). Hundreds of audio teaching tapes and numerous video messages are also available.

- Jim has also authored fourteen complete Study Guides on themes such as *Equipping in the Prophetic, Empower Ministry Training,* and *Blueprints For Prayer* with corresponding tape albums, all of which are used for individual or group study.

You may also receive Jim's monthly e-mail communique call **Vision Cast** and Michal Ann's monthly e-mail devotional called **Women on the Frontlines** by signing in on the Home page of their web site.
Jim is also a contributing writer to *Kairos Magazine* available by subscription.

Visit their web site at **www.jimgoll.com** or **www.mttnweb.com**

For ordering, or for more information, contact:
Ministry to the Nations' Resource Center
at 615-599-5552

Available at your local Christian bookstore.

For more information and sample chapters, visit www.destinyimage.com

RESOURCES
by Lou Engle

The Elijah Revolution

is a movement to see a nation turned back to God through Nazirite consecration, massive fasting and praying, and turning the hearts of the Fathers to the Children and the Children to the Fathers.

Is God speaking to you in dreams?

At **elijahrevolution.com** register to log in, to participate, and to find a place where you can share your dreams and learn to interpret them. Post your own dream or reply to interpret for someone else.

CDs, books, tapes, and videos are all available through Lou's website: **www.elijahrevolution.com**

- **The Contender**
  4-tape series
  The battle of the ages will come down to whose house of prayer will prevail and whose devotion and sacrifice will move Heaven. God is calling His people to *supreme devotion, prophetic intercession* and *massive fasting*.
  Item #C-R . . . . retails @ $21.99

- **Give Me One Praying Student!**
  Video [(60 min) can be produced in Pal version]
  No more bleache bones in the desert, give us the walled cities of the schools of America and the Nations!
  Item #OPS-R . . . . retails @ $20.00

Become an ER partner and sign up for the tape, CD, or video of the month club, which entitles you to 10% off all products.

To purchase products or contact the ministry:
Elijah Revolution, 1539 E. Howard St., Pasadena, CA 91104
Info@elijahrevolution.com

For info about *The Call*, please visit: **www.thecallrevolution.com**

Available at your local Christian bookstore.

Additional copies of this book and other
book titles from DESTINY IMAGE are
available at your local bookstore.

For a complete list of our titles,
visit us at www.destinyimage.com
Send a request for a catalog to:

Destiny Image₍ₐ₎ Publishers, Inc.

P.O. Box 310
Shippensburg, PA 17257-0310

"Speaking to the Purposes of God for This
Generation and for the Generations to Come"

Destiny Image titles
you will enjoy reading